Prai

"*Single* made me feel b

even single right now. It's a warm, joyful book full of solidarity and lots of new ways of looking at single life. I'll be thinking about this book for a while!"

—Radhika Sanghani, author of *30 Things I Love About Myself*

"Nicola Slawson is the authority on building the single life you deserve—and she's written the book that every single woman needs." —Rebecca Reid, author of *Rude*

"Nicola manages to do a rare thing: she shows compassion for single people without pitying them. She celebrates their narrative while also understanding that they might change how they feel about it from one month to the next. And she helps them to search for connection in many different places, as well as to understand themselves better. I wish *Single* existed when I was single."

—Natasha Lunn, author of *Conversations on Love*

"Nicola is a trailblazer. Her work is a vital and necessary contribution to the evolving conversation about relationships." —Vicky Spratt, author of *Tenants*

PENGUIN LIFE

SINGLE

NICOLA SLAWSON is the creator of the cult newsletter *The Single Supplement.* She is passionate about telling human stories—other people's and her own—and is a freelance journalist, writer, and public speaker.

Single

Living a Complete Life on Your Own Terms

NICOLA SLAWSON

life

PENGUIN BOOKS
An imprint of Penguin Random House LLC
1745 Broadway, New York, NY 10019
penguinrandomhouse.com

A Penguin Life Book

Set in Sabon LT Pro by Jouve (UK), Milton Keynes

ISBN 9780143137801 (trade paperback)
ISBN 9780593511916 (ebook)

First published in the United States of America by Viking (Penguin Life), an imprint of Penguin Random House LLC, 2025
Published simultaneously in Great Britain by Headline Home, an imprint of Headline Publishing Group Limited, 2025

Printed in the United States of America
1st Printing

The authorized representative in the EU for product safety and compliance is Penguin Random House Ireland, Morrison Chambers, 32 Nassau Street, Dublin D02 YH68, Ireland, https://eu-contact.penguin.ie.

For all my sisters who read *The Single Supplement* and are part of the community . . . but especially my actual sister, Rachel.

Contents

Introduction: Redefining the Single Experience

One evening around five years ago, I was sitting out on the patio of a beautiful twelfth-century stone coach house in the South of France, looking into the eyes of a woman—a mother—who had just asked me a question that made me falter. She wanted to know what advice I would give to her daughter, who was in her mid-twenties, and who was feeling really sad about being the only one in her friendship group who was single. Her question hit a nerve.

Over the course of the yoga retreat we were both on, I had spoken about being a thirtysomething single woman and how I wanted to be a mum and yet didn't really want to date. For a number of years prior to that moment, that question, I hadn't really let myself think about how I truly felt about my relationship status and, until I'd joined that retreat, I had been trying my hardest to avoid questions about how long I had been single whenever it came up in conversation—which it invariably did. I'd only booked the trip—a combination of yoga and group coaching—because I'd had no one to go on holiday with that year, which I've since learned is a common problem for singles over the age of thirty, as those in relationships are more likely to spend their money on family holidays rather than going away with their mates. When I say that I only realized it was a common problem afterward, this was because my oh-so-charming inner critic had been telling me that the problem was me and that I was probably just too annoying to go on holiday with. The yoga retreat, however, ended up being a brilliant decision. It was the perfect space to open up and be vulnerable—and I didn't realize how much I'd needed that until I was actually there. Yet when this kindhearted woman asked me what I'd say to her daughter, I hesitated. What could I possibly say that could provide any comfort?

I remembered how I had felt in my mid-twenties. From ages twenty to twenty-two, I had been in an incredibly toxic relationship. When that ended, I then jumped into a relationship that led to my ditching my fledgling arts management career and moving to the other side of the world, changing the course of my life forever. When that too ended, I quickly fell head over heels for a man who couldn't love me back. The back-to-back heartbreak of all this had felt like too much to bear. I couldn't understand what I was doing so wrong when others seemed to find romantic love and relationships so easily. As I contemplated this mother's request, I knew that, if I could go back in time and tell twentysomething-year-old me that, so many years on, I still couldn't be more single if I tried, I would have been gutted.

But, I wondered, would I go back and take all those years away? To my surprise, I realized I wouldn't. At some point during all those years I had been single, it had become more of a choice than a last resort. Although I've had flings and flirtations and weird "it's complicated" situationships, I haven't had a proper boyfriend since 2013. Another thing I was surprised to realize was that I've actually been happier than ever. This isn't to say I haven't had moments of feeling down about my relationship status, but my life was—and still is—great.

So I took a deep breath and answered the mother in front of me. I told her that while I would like a partner in the future, some of the absolute best times of my life had happened while I'd been single. My life now was completely unrecognizable from what it had been when I had last used the word "boyfriend." I had moved countries, changed careers, completed a master's degree, won two prestigious scholarships and smashed professional goals. From spontaneous nights out to traveling around Morocco for a month by myself, to moving to Berlin for three months, I had prioritized adventure and having fun. I was healthy. I was surrounded by supportive family and friends. I had my dream job, an active social life and lots of big dreams and ambitions.

I told the woman to tell her daughter exactly that; that I wouldn't go back and take this time away. I'm so grateful for everything I have learned, and she should use this time to take charge of her own happiness and be completely and authentically true to herself.

Why Do We Feel So Bad About Being Single?

The conversation with the mother on the yoga retreat stayed with me, however. I thought about it for months afterward. The question that kept coming back to me was why someone so young should be feeling so bad about being single. Of course it can be painful and lonely to want something you don't have, but if we lived in a world where being single was more acceptable and more celebrated, maybe this girl, who was in the prime of her life, wouldn't feel so bad about being "out of sync" with her friends?

I was older than her, but I related to how she felt, because even though I knew I had a lot of things going for me in my life, I still had this sense that I was somehow doing everything wrong. That my life was wrong. Unnatural, even. Surely it's part of human nature to want to find a mate? Everybody should want that. And yet even though, at the time, I wasn't exactly thrilled about my relationship status, I was also not doing anything to change it. I wondered whether my feelings about being single were more to do with what I thought I should feel as someone without a partner, rather than how I actually felt, and nothing to do with what I actually needed at that time. I've been through the full spectrum of feelings about being single, from sadness to anger to delight and empowerment—but, by and large, society makes us feel like we should only ever be feeling negatively about it, and like it's something rare and different.

Although it can sometimes feel like everyone but you is shacked up with a partner, only around 60% of the UK population reported living in a couple in 2019, according to data from the Office for National Statistics. The majority of these couples were married, while around one in five were cohabiting. It's worth pointing out that this data focuses very much on living situations and official marital status (i.e., so even those who are in long-term relationships are counted as single if they haven't got married or entered into a civil partnership and aren't cohabiting either), which does make it hard to put a figure on how many of the remaining 40% are completely single. We do know, however, that around one in four people are not living in a couple and have never been married or in a civil partnership. More than 7 million Brits live alone. Meanwhile, the data shows that there were also 2.9 million single-parent families recorded that same year, which represents 14.9% of families in the UK.

The fact is that all around the world things are changing. Globally, marriage is in decline while single living is on the rise, according to the 2019 report "Families in a Changing World," released by UN Women. Their research found that female attitudes are changing when it comes to monogamous commitments, and are shifting toward a focus on career goals, self-love and personal growth—and this has led to there being more single women than ever before. So what is all this data telling us? In short, it demonstrates that being single is actually pretty normal. It's certainly not some rare, freakish state.

If being single is not a problem to solve, though, why do so many of us feel like it is? One of the reasons is that, despite the data showing that being single is perfectly normal, society's attitudes haven't yet caught up. We still live in a coupled-up—and very heteronormative—world, where those in monogamous straight relationships are favored and celebrated, while attitudes toward single people or anyone living outside the status quo are mostly negative, with people still expressing a mixture of pity, fear and judgment when finding out someone is unattached.

A scroll through social media while the hit reality-TV show *Love Island* is on air can give us an insight into the way some people feel about those who are single. "There must be something wrong with her if she has never had a boyfriend," one 2019 tweet read. Another said: "He's too picky. This isn't Friend Island!," while another wrote: "You can tell she is just settling. She isn't even trying to hide that she's not into him." And someone else said: "Why are they taking love advice from the one guy who is single? What would he know?" You don't have to be the star of a reality-TV show to recognize those attitudes. I have often been told that I'm being too picky, while also, conversely, being told I should never settle for less than I deserve. Sometimes both these phrases are even uttered in the same conversation by the same people, who don't seem to register that they completely contradict each other.

The media perpetuates the problem too. Before starting my newsletter, *The Single Supplement*, I noticed that content for single people—whether it was books, articles or TV programs—usually centers around dating and trying to stop being single, rather than exploring what it is really like to be unattached in this day and age. All of the articles I came across seemed to assume all single people were miserable and desperate. This just didn't reflect my life.

All too often we single folk are simply forgotten about. A while ago, for example, I read an article that suggested tips for self-care if you were having a bad time. The first thing on the list was to cancel on your friends and "have a cozy night in with your significant other." The writer had obviously not considered that many readers of the magazine would not be able to follow this advice. Not long after, I saw an article in a different magazine featuring tips for saving money, and the first tip was almost identical. It was actually after reading one of these articles—and throwing the magazine across the room in frustration—that I first had the idea for *The Single Supplement*.

The government also plays a part. In the UK, successive chancellors have spoken about "struggling families" and "hard-working families" when announcing new policies. This was particularly hammered home during the pandemic and recent cost-of-living crisis. Yet there are myriad practical concerns, from housing to personal finances, that can be considerably harder to deal with when you're single, and it can feel that the government simply doesn't realize that single people exist. Despite there being millions of single people in our society, those who are not in relationships are often left on the margins. We deserve better.

Reframing Our Single Status

Whether you end up being single for a day or a lifetime, or aren't even single at all, we all deserve to be liberated from toxic and deeply embedded attitudes toward our relationship status, and what that does or doesn't mean about who we are and what our value is. I also believe the shame people feel about being single and the narratives around what it means to live happily ever after mean that many of the issues that affect single people are overlooked. It stops people from living to their fullest potential, because they can have a tendency to put things they want to do on hold and feel like they are waiting for their lives to properly start. Worse still, it drives others to make terrible decisions, either to stay in toxic relationships or settle for less-than-ideal partners. The recent rise of the incel movement is also a nasty development—these disaffected young men believe that being single is the very worst thing a person can suffer through.

Meanwhile, and more encouragingly, the so-called single positivity movement has exploded in the last few years, and each time I see a single person standing in their own power and shouting about how liberating it is to be single, and how they've realized it's possible to be both single and happy, it feels like I'm part of a beautiful rebellion. I want that for more of us, but, equally, I'm also not one to sugarcoat the challenges nor force any toxic positivity down people's throats.

For me, the single positivity movement isn't even about being happily single. It's about smashing the stigma that single people are sad, pathetic individuals. It's about demonstrating that being single doesn't automatically equate with being miserable. It's about emphasizing the idea that we have the right to enjoy our lives as much as possible without feeling like we are "in waiting" or "behind" or "on the shelf."

After I began owning my own singleness—first with an opinion piece I was persuaded to write by the *HuffPost* Lifestyle desk, and then with my newsletter, I noticed things begin to shift. My confidence grew, and after years of shame and secretiveness, I finally felt like I was being my most authentic self. For a long time, I hadn't acknowledged my single status and felt mortified about the idea of talking about it on social media, where ex-boyfriends and potential love interests might see it, as though it was a dark and shameful secret. But when I first began talking about all this, about my feelings about my relationship status, it quickly felt like a weight had been lifted from my shoulders, like I had whipped off the mask I'd been hiding behind. I also began making decisions that were best for me, such as leaving London and moving back to my hometown. Prior to this I had put off making big decisions, perpetually postponing them until an elusive point in the future when I would theoretically "settle down," which, of course, I assumed would happen with a partner.

Who Is This Book For?

As I was editing the first draft of this book, I realized I'd been single for a decade. When I first became single all those years ago, I never would have guessed I would ever feel confident and comfortable enough to write just how long I've been single anywhere, let alone in an actual book, which feels somewhat akin to tattooing the word "single" on my forehead. But I'm motivated by a desire to change things so no one else feels embarrassed or ashamed of their single status—and I can only do this by leading by example and writing about my experience.

Over the last few years I have also spoken to hundreds of single people about how they really feel about their own unattached lives. My goal has been to truly explore the single experience in all its guises, from those who are newly broken up to those who have been single for decades. From those who lost their loved ones through death and those through divorce. From those who have always been single to those who are experiencing it for the very first time. I have also spoken to a few coupled-up people about the transition from single life to being in a relationship.

But there are so many ways I could have approached this book. It could have been a political and feminist manifesto, or an examination of social and historical context, or many other things besides. But I decided to focus on people's stories—my own and others—as a way to shine a light on the highs and lows of being single, and so that, hopefully, you, my reader, feel less alone.

I could have also focused on all single people, but instead chose to focus on single women and non-binary people in the main. This was partly because, otherwise, the book would have to be double the size, involve a lot more interviews, and would have taken even longer to write than it did, but also because I don't believe I'm the best person for the job. I'd absolutely love to see a similar book in bookshops covering the single male experience from the perspective of a man. Nevertheless, men are welcome here—just as they are in the Facebook group I run: I hope you find some comfort in these pages.

Whether you are long-term single, recently single, keen not to be, happy to be, considering becoming, voluntarily, involuntarily, and so on, I want more than anything for this book to help you feel confident about talking openly about being single without feeling shame, and also help you get to a point where you genuinely don't care what other people think of your relationship status. I think that by releasing some of that shame around it, we'd all be a little more at ease.

Sometimes being single has been tricky for me. Sometimes I've wondered what's "wrong" with me. Sometimes I've felt lonely. Sometimes I've longed for romantic love. But I also know that I have built a beautiful, colorful, vibrant life for myself. It's a life I didn't sit around waiting to make happen until I found a partner to do it with. While not perfect, it's the kind of life we all deserve, and one that I hope you will feel is within your reach whether you are single for a couple of months or for the rest of your life.

ONE

Getting Over Heartbreak and Learning to Be Newly Single

The worst heartbreak of my life happened when I was a long way from home. I was twenty-five years old, living in South Korea, and my boyfriend, James, and I had broken up for the first time. It was a sudden and acrimonious breakup. One September night, while out drinking, we got into a blazing row. Overnight, we went from living in each other's pockets to not speaking to each other. In fact, James assured me he would never speak to me ever again. The breakup, unfortunately, also coincided with several other things that were happening in my life at the time—friendship falling-outs and my granddad's death—and so it felt like my whole world was imploding.

The reason I was in South Korea in the first place was because James had asked me to go. We had met in England a couple of years before and had become best friends, until one night when we kissed. We'd only been seeing each other for a couple months when he suggested that we find jobs in South Korea, teaching English at private academies, who would pay for our flights and our apartments. We didn't even need any qualifications. I'd been desperate to see the world—having not been able to afford a gap year—and was head over heels in love with him, so it seemed like a no-brainer.

After the breakup, and despite everything that happened, I really did not want to leave South Korea. But in order to stay, I had to hang on to my visa, which meant I had to keep working. There were definitely no mental health days available to help me through.

The fact we were so far from home was also what made the breakup so hard. In South Korea, James felt like family. We were each other's link to home. Now, we weren't even talking. I felt broken. I had thought he was the love of my life. How often do you meet someone you'd be willing to move to the other side of the world for—after just a couple of months seeing each other—I would reason.

I was a nervous wreck in the weeks that followed. I was a ball of jittery, fearful energy. I felt raw, as if my skin had been peeled off. I was twitchy. I missed him so much and felt like I couldn't survive without him. All the usual clichés. I couldn't eat. I couldn't sleep. I cried constantly, and sometimes the tears would be flowing and I'd only notice when I realized my pillow was sodden or my face was wet.

The nervous feeling was the worst part. I couldn't sit still. Anytime I was home alone, I'd find myself dwelling on what had happened and obsessively refreshing Facebook—the social media du jour at the time. I ended up going to the gym a lot. I'd sit for ages on the exercise bike, crying my eyes out while all the gym regulars worked out around me. None of them paid me much attention and I didn't really care even if they did. I just sat there absolutely hammering the pedals as the front of my T-shirt became increasingly damp through a mixture of sweat and tears.

One evening I was in my tiny flat, having what I now know was a panic attack, when Helen, a friend of mine, called. I grasped my phone like it was a life raft. She'd been calling to arrange going for dinner, but heard my raggedy gasping breath and knew immediately what was happening. She gave me advice that has stuck with me ever since. She told me I just had to make it through the next hour. She suggested I make a note of what time it would be in one hour's time and just remind myself of that time when I was struggling. When the clock hit that time, I could repeat the activity and just try to make it until the hour after that. If I was really flat-out panicking, as I had been when she called, I could even break it down further into minutes instead.

For the next week or so, I followed this advice. At work, where I taught English lessons to children aged two to eighteen, I marked the time in fifteen-minute interludes on the edge of my lesson plans. If I started to feel like I might cry or panic, I would look down at the time and see how long I had left. When I reached the allotted time, I'd congratulate myself that I'd made it without breaking down. As I began to adjust to life without James, the urge to burst into tears began to fade.

Soon after this it was Chuseok, the South Korean national holiday to celebrate harvest time, and I had five days to fill, which felt daunting. Luckily, some friends asked if I wanted to go with them to Seoul, the capital city. The change of scenery helped, but I still felt like a walking exposed nerve. But at some point on that trip—I have no recollection of how or where—I acquired a copy of Elizabeth Gilbert's *Eat Pray Love*. The film adaptation starring Julia Roberts had just been released, which is probably why I picked it up. I vividly remember reading her raw and honest descriptions of the messy but intense relationship she'd fallen into directly after leaving her husband. I was lying on the lower bunk of the bed in the youth hostel where we were staying and experiencing these waves of realization about the nature of my relationship with my ex-boyfriend—and feeling so "seen." I was not alone, I realized.

I know it makes me a massive walking cliché, but I will

forever be grateful for *Eat Pray Love*, that it was there for me in my hour of need. I hung on to the book like it was my bible. That's the thing about heartbreaks: in the moment, they feel so unique to you that you think nobody else could possibly understand how it feels. But the truth is heartbreaks are universal. It's something we will all experience at some point or another—or if you are anything like me, at many points.

The Science of Heartbreaks

There is actually a scientific reason why I felt as bad as I felt back in South Korea—and why you may be feeling this way now, if you're going through a breakup. Comedian and writer Rosie Wilby, author of *The Breakup Monologues* and host of a podcast of the same name, has become somewhat of an expert on breakups, and she enjoys delving into the science behind why we feel the way we do.

"You felt really weird when you broke up because you were literally addicted to that person," she told me, when I interviewed her for this chapter. "When we are first in love or lust, all these very exciting happy chemicals are whizzing around the brain when we see them and when we're around them. We are feeling the effects of dopamine and oxytocin."

Dopamine is a neurotransmitter associated with our reward systems, whereas oxytocin is often known as the "cuddle" chemical, because it bonds us to others. Mothers who've just given birth will have a rush of oxytocin, for example. We also feel those chemicals after we've had sex, or had some kind of intimacy with somebody.

"Later in our relationship, our brain releases these opiates; so we really are becoming addicted to this person," Rosie says. "There were people who were studying the effects of drug withdrawal who noticed that people who were going through a breakup were experiencing all the same things as those coming off drugs. They were feeling that twitchiness, that inability to concentrate, that loss of appetite, that inability to sleep or be calm or stay still. There were so many parallels with drug withdrawal that they realized that, actually, a person who is newly single after a breakup is going through a withdrawal. It's very much the same chemical-type process.

"We get so used to something and so acclimatized to a person's smell, sound, their voice, and suddenly all these little transmitters and synapses in our brain are suddenly not getting that hit, so they're like, 'Oh, where is it?' and you feel weird."

One researcher who has looked into this is Helen Fisher, a biological anthropologist who studies the effects of love on the brain. Using functional MRI scans, she has identified striking similarities between losing a loved one and quitting an addiction. She found activity in the brain regions associated with craving and obsession, as well as in the nucleus accumbens, which is widely recognized for being part of the "reward circuit" of the brain and therefore plays a major role in addictive behavior. There was also activity in the region associated with physical pain and the anxiety that goes along with physical pain.

This all makes so much sense, and actually makes me feel better for how awful I was feeling back then. That terrible experience wasn't the end of the story for me and James, though. After around six weeks of torture, we ended up getting back together. But by the following summer it was time to say goodbye again. I was heading off to Italy to run summer English camps for children and he was off to Eastern Europe, to teach English there. We went our separate ways, and had mutually agreed it would mean the end of our relationship—for good this time.

Learning to Let Go

Before heading to Italy, I decided to have one last adventure in Asia, using the bonus I received at the end of my teaching contract in South Korea. I headed to Malaysia and did a week-long yoga retreat. Malaysia and then Italy: *Eat Pray Love* had clearly influenced me more than I realized at the time. In Langkawi, where I did the yoga retreat, I tried to push down my tumultuous feelings and pretend I was just a normal person and not the husk of one that I actually felt myself to be. After the retreat in what felt like paradise, I flew to Italy, which was when reality finally set in about what I'd just lost.

Unlike the autumn heartbreak, this separation had been amicable, which somehow made it sadder, in a way. I Skyped or instant messaged James every chance I got, however, so at least I wasn't going cold turkey this time. Even so, I still felt his absence in every single decision I made. Things like choosing where to go for dinner and even what to eat when I got there felt almost impossible. I was also navigating a new country and adjusting back to Europe after a year in Asia, and I felt panicky trying to navigate such a sprawling city, alone, without knowing any Italian and without him there to calm me down. I seemed to have lost—to steal a phrase from parenting books—the ability to self-soothe. I felt as if I was missing a crucial part of myself. In short, I didn't feel whole.

This was something the *Vogue* columnist Annie Lord experienced when she went through her first heartbreak, a subject she analyzes in her bestselling memoir, *Notes on Heartbreak*.

Annie had been with her boyfriend for five years when, seemingly out of the blue, he unceremoniously broke up with her in the street following a meal out. The next day, in a state of shock, she decided to travel home to see her parents in Leeds. It was on the train that she actually felt her heart break, as the reaction had been delayed by the unexpectedness of the breakup. It was her first experience of heartbreak and the pain shocked her. In the weeks that followed, as friends and family rallied around, she recalled typing "Can you die from heartbreak?" into Google.

I interviewed Annie, who said: "The thing I found most painful to get my head around was this idea that it was done and finished, and that one day there'll be a me that doesn't care about him anymore."

Like Annie, the thing I have always found most difficult to overcome during a breakup is the idea that you have to suddenly stop caring about your former partner and stop being part of their lives. Where does all that love go?

"After a while I realized you'll actually always care," Annie told me. "It's just the way you care kind of changes. Now I find it kind of nice. Sometimes I'll make myself upset and think about it all in a kind of sentimental way, kind of like picking a scab to see if it still hurts a little bit. The other day I was walking and listening to Lana Del Rey and just thinking of him, but I was in control of it. It's a long process."

Reframing the meaning of what success and failure looks like in relationships also helped her: "A friend of mine was saying it was so sad that a couple hadn't worked out, but

I don't think that's necessarily a very good way of looking at it. It did work for a time and then it stopped working. That doesn't mean it's a failure, because it didn't go on forever—and nothing lasts forever anyway."

Annie echoed something I thought a lot about, back when I was doing that yoga retreat in Langkawi following my breakup with James. At the retreat, I hadn't mentioned my breakup to the yoga teachers—a Malaysian woman named Meng Foong and her Irish husband, Marc—but I could tell Meng Foong, who remains one of the wisest people I've ever met, could see right through me. I wasn't fooling her. In fact, I knew for sure she was on to me on the day she taught me about the Buddhist concept of impermanence during one lesson.

"Think about it," she said. "Nothing is permanent. To feel happier and more at ease, you have to learn to let go of your attachment to everything." Thinking of James, I asked her how I could let go when it felt so painful and difficult and, frankly, terrifying. As I asked her this, I was holding my water bottle in one hand.

"You see the way you are holding on to the bottle there," she responded. "Think of all the muscles involved in holding it and how they are tensing and contracting to enable you to grip it and hold its weight. Now put it down. What's happened to your hand and arm?"

"They have relaxed," I replied.

"Exactly. It's difficult to hold on to things and it's painful to hold on to the ones that don't serve us. All that tension and struggle disappears when we let it go," she said.

This is very much easier said than done, but I have returned to her words over and over since she said them, more than twelve years ago, and they have applied to so many situations, from jobs that aren't working out to toxic friendships, and, of course, to all those situations with love interests where you are ignoring all the red flags and desperately trying to make it work. Letting it go feels hard, but holding on is so much harder.

Why Short-Lived Love Is Sometimes So Painful

While it's true that nothing is permanent, this is even more true for some relationships than others, because they are only short-lived. Weirdly, the heartbreaks that follow these brief relationships can be just as painful as long relationships, if not more so. This is something that has come up both with friends and with members of *The Single Supplement* community. People are often taken by surprise at how heartbroken it's possible to feel following the end of something short-term or even after just a few dates. Some have told me that they felt worse after these kinds of relationships than they did when long-term ones failed.

If I were to rank my heartbreaks, my second most painful was with someone I went on a grand total of four dates and one weekend away with. To be fair, they were by far the most romantic dates of my life. It felt magical. I was giddy with excitement. After our weekend away, which had been—I thought—amazing, we arranged to go for dinner. A romantic dinner, I thought. He had other ideas, however, and had invited me in order to dump me. Neither of us expected the strong reaction I had. One minute he was saying he didn't see a future for us and, the next second, I was weeping big fat tears and—I am not exaggerating—I could not stop. We had to leave. It was mortifying. And I was just as perplexed as he was. Even though I was completely smitten, how could I be so upset by such a short-term thing?

Now that I'm older and have seen it happen to others, I have a better understanding of what was going on. When things are short-lived, they can be harder to overcome because we haven't experienced that initial shine rubbing off them before they are over. If we had got together properly and then broken up, the rose-tinted glasses would already have come off and I would have been aware of all his flaws and faults. In something short-lived, you're still in the honeymoon phase, full of optimism. You've probably been imagining a shiny future together. So you aren't just losing this person you haven't known that long, but also this potential future life. It may have just been a fantasy, but it doesn't mean it doesn't hurt to lose it.

Being the Dumper, Not the Dumpee

Heartbreak is not just reserved for those who have been dumped either. I remember how sad I was when I realized the boyfriend I had when I lived in Spain (which is where I ended up after my summer in Italy) had moved on after I broke up with him. It made it feel final. It didn't help that he hadn't told me about his new girlfriend and just casually brought her along to my leaving do when I was going back to the UK. I knew I had made the right decision to end our relationship, and yet I questioned myself because I didn't expect to be so upset.

I'm not alone in seemingly feeling sadder by the end of the relationship as the dumper rather than the dumpee. One of the members of *The Single Supplement* community, Josephine Scott, a forty-two-year-old clinical psychologist who lives in Norwich, told me what it was like in the immediate aftermath of her marriage ending, which had been her decision. She and her partner had been married for nine years, together for eleven, had two young children, and owned their house together.

"I felt a roller coaster of emotions when it ended, but mostly grief. I remember, after I'd moved out, it was the Easter Bank Holiday weekend and a beautiful day, and the children weren't with me," she tells me. "As I'd been the one to end the relationship, I felt like I should be the one to move out. My rented house was a dark terraced property, and not what I would have chosen. I sat on the back of an armchair, as close to the window as possible, eating a chocolate egg I'd bought myself and in floods of tears—imagining all the happy families out there enjoying the sun.

"My ex appeared unaffected by my departure, and I found that very hard to take. It was almost a physical pain a lot of the time in those first few months, and I measured my recovery in terms of how frequently I'd cried that day, week or month."

A Note on Relationship Trauma

I think it's important to note that some heartbreaks have a long tail because they are intermingled with trauma. A few years after I first decided to be single, I found myself sitting in a small nondescript box room in a random office block in Kings Cross, London, in front of a middle-aged woman with kind eyes. This woman was a relationship coach, who I had been embarrassed to tell any of my friends about, but who I'd come to see as a bit of an experiment. I was having a hard time with my mental health and believed all my problems would be solved if only I could get myself a boyfriend.

Within about fifteen minutes of our session beginning, I was crying so much I couldn't catch my breath. I felt totally blindsided. I had thought the experience might be quite fun—or at least interesting. Instead, I was having what felt like a breakdown as the coach watched on. All she had done was ask me to go through my relationship history. It started off okay, but things took a turn for the worse as I recalled a university boyfriend, the last serious relationship I'd had before James. He'd been so romantic at first, but our relationship had increasingly become toxic in multiple ways and, I now realized, this had left its mark.

For years I had pushed what happened down, explaining away his behavior, and I'd certainly never considered myself a victim in any way. In fact, it wasn't until I read Marian Keyes' *This Charming Man*, a novel where one of the characters slowly realizes her ex was a domestic abuser, that I first started to rethink experiences I'd had over the years that had certain parallels. Some people might not understand why someone who has experienced a toxic relationship, let alone domestic abuse, as in the Keyes novel, would ever need a book, and a fictional one at that, to help them understand what happened to them, but such is the nature of the beast. Like Lola in the book, I was almost brainwashed. I had repeatedly dismissed the actions of men who hadn't treated me well over the years, explained them away, and refused to see what was clear as day to anyone else. I can still remember the hairs on the back of my neck standing on end as I read the all too familiar story.

Back in the coach's office, I managed to calm myself enough to look back up at her. She thanked me for being so open and honest, and then she carefully said this next line, which would change everything for me: "I'm sorry, but I'm not going to be able to take you on as a client," she said gently. "From what you have told me and how these experiences have affected you, I believe you are traumatized by these relationships, and I'm not qualified to help people through trauma. I don't think you are ready for a relationship and think it's best if you seek help and, perhaps, therapy."

At first I felt like I'd been slapped. Great, I thought, I'm being rejected by a relationship coach. You couldn't make this up. Then the word "traumatized" reached me and those hurt feelings disappeared. Suddenly it all made sense. It was like someone had opened a door that had been there all along, but that I hadn't noticed. I already know this, I realized. I just needed someone else to say it out loud.

I finally felt like I had an explanation for why I hadn't been able to get over things in my past, when all around me friends and peers seemed to be able to get over heartbreak easily. I turned the word over in my head. Nowadays it's used daily. All over social media, people are owning the word "trauma" and discussing how being traumatized in the past has affected them. But even just a few years ago, you rarely heard that word. I associated PTSD with soldiers coming back from war—I didn't think I had a right to the diagnosis. And even now, after professionals have agreed with her assessment, I still feel some imposter syndrome about using the word "trauma."

*

In the years following my meeting with the relationship coach, I did a lot of self-work. I was incredibly lucky to receive lots of therapy for free on the NHS, including two years of psychotherapy. I learned to meditate. I completed The Artist's Way, a three-month self-discovery course aimed at creatives, which I found very healing. I really began to enjoy being single. I realized that, prior to seeing the coach, I had just focused on what I was lacking. I was comparing myself so much to my friends and equating feeling depressed in general with feeling sad about not having a partner. In reality, they are two different things, which should be obvious, as plenty of people in relationships also struggle with mental health problems.

Sometimes I let myself believe that, thanks to my early relationship trauma, I'm somehow permanently broken and I've lost that part of myself that desires a relationship in the way other people seem to. Maybe there is some truth in this; it certainly makes entering a relationship potentially more high stakes for me than it might be for others who have only had more "normal" experiences. But there are plenty of people who are in relationships despite having experienced similar traumas. Some, I know, are drawn to the safe bet, getting into relationships in order to feel secure and, in some cases, settling even if they aren't in love. But there are also, of course, many cases of people who have found happiness in loving romantic relationships following trauma. It impacts everyone differently.

I have now reached a fairly stable equilibrium after those years of disastrous relationships, though, and it's understandable for me to want to maintain that. In fact, it's logical, really. Things have shifted, however. A few years ago I wrote in my newsletter that I was terrified to get into a new relationship. As I came to write this chapter, I was going to include something similar, but then I realized it was no longer true. I'm no longer afraid. Even so, I'm still not in a hurry to find The One, and I think that's okay. One day I will be. Or maybe I won't. Either way, I know I will be fine.

Surviving the Loss of a Partner

Of course, one of the most painful losses we can endure is not due to a relationship breaking down but because our partner dies. I wanted to ask women who have been through this about how they coped. While I was writing this book, I became addicted to the BBC TV show *The Traitors*. Like a lot of the viewers of the show's first season, I developed a soft spot for the oldest member of the cast, seventy-three-year-old retired civil servant Andrea Addison.

Viewers of the program delighted in the friendships Andrea made with younger cast members, who seemed to see her as a grandmother figure. On social media she was hailed as a gay icon, after she opened up about the loss of her partner of twenty-six years.

After you get over the initial sharpness of a heartbreak or grief, you're faced with a new challenge: adjusting to single life. I wanted to speak to Andrea because she had had to recalibrate her life after being with her partner for such a long time in addition to dealing with her grief. I asked her how she managed.

Andrea, who lives in rural Belgium, with farm animals and land to look after, said: "It was very tough to adjust when she died. It is still very tough. It's tough emotionally. It's tough economically. It's tough. Today is a beautiful day outside, so it is less tough, but sometimes it's a ghastly day or you don't feel very well but you're still just there alone, and you have to do everything yourself."

Because of the responsibilities she has with the animals she owns, she hasn't been able to stay in bed when grief gets the better of her. "I can't just say to myself, 'I'm not gonna get up today,' but this is actually a good thing because there's no choice in it. That's not to say it isn't hard, though, and there are times when I find it overwhelmingly hard."

In these moments, she usually calls a friend and just chats to them, although she doesn't usually admit how she is actually feeling. "Just talking to them about their day helps and makes me feel less alone. That's a technique, if you like," she says. "When you live alone, it's good to remind ourselves that we are still part of life. We still need to embrace life and to make sure that we're feeling alive. There are times when you want to shut yourself up and cry or whatever, and that's okay, because that's also part of life."

I asked if she had any advice for those who are going through grief or the loss of a loved one. She told me it was important not to minimize your grief or sadness.

She says: "It may go on for a very long time, but that's okay. Try to be open to new experiences. Think of things you like doing, such as playing cards or doing a sport, and arrange to do it with someone or join a club. Moving your body is a good idea.

"Think about doing some volunteering—I help refugees, which helps put things in perspective and gets you out. It helps you connect and communicate, which is so important. There will be times when you want to sit at home, but try not to let yourself do that too much."

Not letting yourself wallow at home is such good advice. For Andrea, that involved signing up to that brand new TV show that involved weeks spent in rural Scotland with a large group of others, all trying to beat each other to win a cash prize. She signed up because she fancied an adventure, and I love that she chose to do that for herself.

How to Feel Better in the Early Days

Going on an adventure, big or small, is a really good way to feel better in general, I have found. In Italy, following my final breakup with James, I threw myself into traveling around the country. There are other kinds of adventures, though. Annie Lord went out clubbing with her friends a lot following her breakup. She also started dating and having sex almost immediately. Rosie Wilby, meanwhile, turned her pain into art by creating a comedy show about how her ex-girlfriend had dumped her by email. She also spent lots of quality time with her friends. And her research suggests spending time with animals, as Andrea does, helps too, as the cuddle hormone gets released when you pet and hold them.

Quality time alone can also be really healing. In *Eat Pray Love*, Elizabeth Gilbert talks about moving into a one-bedroom apartment by herself. She says the experience brought "a nascent interior shift" and that she began to feel like "a self-governing individual" again. In her lowest moments, she was still able to enjoy the time alone, and what she says next is a good way to approach life when newly alone. She writes: "I was actually feeling kind of delighted about all the compartments of time and space that were appearing in my days, during which I could ask myself the radical new question: 'What do you want to do, Liz?'" At first she answered the question cautiously. "I would only allow myself to express little baby-step wants. Like: I want to go to a Yoga class. I want to leave this party early, so I can go home and read a novel. I want to buy myself a new pencil box. Then there would always be that one weird answer, same every time: I want to learn how to speak Italian."

What she said about becoming a self-governing individual reminds me of something the late, great bell hooks, author of *All About Love*, wrote: "Knowing how to be solitary is central to the art of loving. When we can be alone, we can be with others without using them as a means of escape."

Being newly single can mean you have to learn to be comfortable doing things alone. This can be scary and anxiety-inducing if it's been a long time since you've had to be alone. Journalist and podcaster Francesca Specter used to hate being on her own so much that she would do absolutely anything to avoid it. She felt that being unable to be by herself was a character trait of hers and, for many years, she didn't try to change this. But as the serious relationship she was in began to falter, she realized she was only hanging on to it for fear of being alone, which was not a good enough reason to stay in an unhappy partnership.

She and her ex had been in the process of moving in together when they split up, which left Francesca living alone for the first time. In an interview for my newsletter, she told me that, at first, she was "scrambling around" to find any way to avoid being alone in the flat, including booking up every single night of the week with dates or time with friends, even saying yes to things she didn't really want to do.

"Rather than giving myself what I really needed, which was time to myself in my flat, I was trying to do anything to run away from it," she told me.

In January 2019, Francesca made a new year's resolution to learn to spend some time alone and to enjoy it. She began to share her experiences and it snowballed from there. Now she is actually most known for advocating for enjoying time alone, whether or not you are in a relationship. That new year's resolution spawned her book, *Alonement*, a podcast of the same name and a community of people committed to carving out and savoring alone time.

Like Elizabeth Gilbert, Francesca started small. At first she took herself for brunch at her favorite local spot, which was something she had always wanted to do with her ex-boyfriend but never did, because he liked to sleep in on the weekend.

"I'd always be hanging around waiting for him, which I really shouldn't have done. When I decided to spend more time alone, I decided to do the one thing I really wanted to do on Saturdays . . . I also started journaling. I had a space to talk to myself and build myself up again and create a sense of me-ness."

Annie Lord had a similar realization, about just how much she had relied on her ex-boyfriend and how she hadn't ever really learned to be independent: "When I was with my ex, I had built myself around him. I was so reliant on him. This is something I realized existed before him. I had been like that in friendships too. I've always been quite needy and easily led," she said.

"Since the breakup and being on my own, I've been trying to be a bit more self-sufficient. I went on holiday to Greece, and that was really nice because it did prove to me that I really liked spending time on my own. Even just getting a flight on my own made me feel good. I just felt really independent."

If you are currently going through a heartbreak, all of this may seem a long way off, and you may also be comparing yourself to others who may seem, from the outside, to get over people faster than you. If you are struggling, don't forget to be kind to yourself. Most of my heartbreaks have taken an inordinately long time to get over. I have never been able to jump from one relationship to another. Allow yourself time to grieve and sit with your feelings.

Looking back, I now know each of my heartbreaks took as long to get over as they were meant to. In some cases, as discussed, there was a lot more than just heartbreak going on. Sometimes things are just complicated and you need to process what happened. Focus on yourself and on rebuilding your life.

There is this pervading myth that, in order to prove to the world and yourself you are over someone, you have to get with someone else. Deciding to be single simply because you want to be for a while—or forever—is also a legitimate choice. For others, finding love again is a priority. There is no right or wrong way to cope. But if you are going through heartbreak now, or are grappling with trauma, please believe me when I say: you won't feel this way forever. Things will shift and adjust and, one day, you might find it's not quite as painful as before.

Breakup To-Do List

I asked members of the Facebook community I run for what they would put on a to do list for the freshly single and newly brokenhearted. Here's what they said:

Have a good cry—or scream

"Allow yourself the time to process and feel sad if you need to, whether that's eating ice cream in bed or just going outside and screaming." —Lauren

Go for a long walk

"Just the repetitive act of putting one foot in front of the other seemed to help." —Sarah

Create a breakup playlist

"Falling to sleep to music gave me something to focus on and helped to stop my mind drifting and overplaying things in my head and torturing myself with whys, ifs, buts." —Debbie

Put the radio on

"There is nothing worse than being alone following a breakup, but you may not want to see other people for a while. Put the radio on. A friendly voice in your ear is always welcome." —Paul

Buy yourself something wonderful or get your nails and hair done

"Remind yourself that brighter days are ahead." —Katherine

Go out dancing with friends

"It sounds counterintuitive, if you're not feeling joyful enough to dance, but dancing always makes me feel better." —Jane

Distract yourself

"What got me through was watching videos on YouTube and doing online meditation courses, etc. I organized my life and set goals using goal planner journals and I dragged myself to events. Distraction was key." —Moira

Get into a new TV show or find comfort in an old one

"I binge watched all nine seasons of *How I Met Your Mother*, back to back, in about two weeks. It gave me space to switch my brain off." —Sue

Exercise

"Moving your body definitely helps! For me, it was cycling." —Yaneva

Find someone to have sex with

“It took me a long time to get back to me after my twenty-two-year-long marriage ended. But the best thing I was told was a quote from (I think) Mae West: the best way to get over a man [or woman] is to get under another.” —Lisa W.

Go on holiday

“One friend went on a group tour to Cuba—for salsa, but she also ended up getting ‘jiggy’ with one of the instructors.” —Mina

Make new friends

“Google meet-up groups in the area you live and make new friendships in order to start your new chapter.” —Judith

Be patient

“An American lady once saw me crying and just said ‘Keep traveling through your feelings, really feel your feelings.’ Embrace the sadness until you’re through.” —Sarah

TWO

Not All Single People Are Created Equal

During one of the most challenging periods of my life—when I'd run out of money and was about to be kicked out of a short-term sublet, leaving me with nowhere to live in the last months of my master's course—a friend said to me: "But why don't you just dip into your savings?" The friend in question was incredibly well off and from a privileged background. She couldn't comprehend that I would have to leave London, move back home with my parents in Shropshire, and drop out of the course, thereby jettisoning my dreams of becoming a journalist. She simply didn't know that not everyone has the luxury of savings.

The fact was that not only did I not have any savings, I was also badly in debt and couldn't even afford the minimum payments, so I was racking up fees and fines and fielding scary phone calls (until I finally spoke to someone who suggested I go onto a debt payment plan). On Saturdays I'd visit the noisy and busy East Street Market in southeast London, which was near the flat I was staying in. It was no middle-class farmer's style market, but similar to the kind you see on *EastEnders*. Consequently, the stall owners wouldn't mind waiting as I counted out coins to buy potatoes, carrots and onions. Afterward I'd head to Aldi to get lentils and other ingredients. Then I'd go home and make a big batch of vegetarian shepherd's pie to see me through the week. I'd take tea bags to uni and pay 50p for hot water, unless the barista took pity on me and gave it to me for free. I'd walk for miles alone in the dark because taxis were well out of my budget. A constant weight of dread hung over me. Whenever I had to pay for something, I would pray my card wouldn't be declined.

To add insult to injury, this wasn't happening when I was in my early twenties, when it feels more socially acceptable to be skint. I'd just turned thirty. So while I was struggling through my attempt to change careers and retrain, most of my best friends were earning decent wages, getting promotions and beginning to settle down with their partners. Prior to starting the course, I'd make self-deprecating jokes about being an intern at twenty-nine and how I was regressing. I'd found the whole thing funny at first, but the joke got old the more my financial woes worsened. I felt humiliated that I'd got myself in this mess at a time when I felt I should have had all my shit together. And I felt incredibly behind when it came to the milestones we're all supposed to hit.

I was also single and had no boyfriend to shack up with and share the bills with. It pains me to admit that I considered getting together with someone—anyone—just to do this with, share finances. Maybe, if I hadn't been so busy juggling my course with work, I would have actually tried this approach, but dating is a time-consuming business. Besides, I wouldn't have been able to afford to go out on dates anyway.

One of the lowest points was when I asked my mum if I could borrow £20 to see me through to my next pay check. But when I went to withdraw it, I left it in the cash machine and walked off without it. When I realized and rushed back in the rain, it had already been taken by someone before it could be sucked back into the machine. I burst into tears and crumpled into the wall. I felt so much shame in that moment that a horrible little thought flashed through my mind: "I'd be better off dead," I thought. Yet, on the upside, when I got robbed in Elephant and Castle tube station, there was no money for them to steal inside my shabby wallet, and even my cards had fallen out of it just before it was nicked.

Every night in bed I would run through the options in my head. My parents had done as much as they could. They had lent me money to cover three month's rent in my sublet, as well as money to pay for my Oyster card, but weren't able to help anymore. The timing couldn't have been worse to ask even for that. My dad, up until a few months prior, had been a mechanic, but was now unable to work after what we later learned was a small stroke, but which at the time was undiagnosed and a medical mystery, leaving him unable to claim benefits or access his pension. It was clear I needed to give the money I'd borrowed back. This wasn't a handout. Meanwhile, my credit rating was so low I couldn't borrow any more money from a bank either. I had no one else to ask.

The worst option open to me, as I saw it, was to drop out and move home, as it meant the previous eighteen months of sacrifice would have been wasted. I could have tried to get another job, but that would have likely meant the end of my student life anyway, as the MA I was doing—which had been paid for in full when I landed the prestigious Scott Trust Bursary—was intensive and full-on. It was difficult enough to find time for the very flexible part-time job I did have. In fact, when I complained to the head of the course about a seminar being changed to a different time last minute, meaning I had to miss an important meeting at work, I was told the course was full time and I shouldn't have a job while doing it anyway. It should come as no surprise that most of the other people on the course were from wealthy backgrounds, or at least had grown up in London and so could stay in their family homes and not have to worry about paying rent. Others could live with boyfriends and girlfriends.

I finally got myself out of the mess by making an emotional visit to the student welfare office, after which I was awarded a hardship grant by the university. I used that money to sublet a cheap room on a houseboat for two months. By the time the course was finishing up and the sublet was over, I was finally beginning to earn more money but still not enough. I turned to a mixture of sofa-surfing and house sitting, until I finally saved the money for a deposit and first month's rent. After two years of instability and stress, I became a lodger in a small room in a council flat, and it was from there that I began to get my foot firmly wedged in the door of journalism, and eventually began earning enough that I actually had to pay tax.

That period of my life was fairly traumatic and has stayed with me. I had to make hard decisions about what I could afford and felt powerless and insecure and often afraid. The whole experience left me with quite a lot of anxiety around money and housing.

Nevertheless, I am conscious I am also privileged in many ways. If worse had come to worse, I could have left the course and moved back to Shrewsbury, as my parents had a spare room and were willing to take me in. Some people's family homes are too small to accommodate them as adults, while others are estranged from their families, meaning they don't have that in-built safety net.

I also had friends willing to let me crash at theirs in the short term, and a sister who, at one point, came to visit me from her home in Cornwall and promptly took me to the supermarket so she could buy me some groceries, and then to Nando's for a meal out. I wasn't alone. I wouldn't have ended up on the streets, and although there were times when I would go to bed hungry, I wouldn't have starved. Not everyone is as lucky. I also don't have physical disabilities, and I am white, so I had advantages when it came to accessing support and landing work and other opportunities that others may have struggled to get.

Surviving on a Low Income When Alone

The simple fact is not all single people are created equal. I think it's important to recognize this, because as much as I advocate for embracing your single status, it's easy for me to say, given the privileges I was born with (white, able-bodied and from a loving family, to name a few) and the position I am now in financially and in my career. So many can be unaware of their privilege, though. When I shared an article about how there was nowhere affordable for women to rent alone, some people took it upon themselves to tell me that this must be wrong, because they themselves could afford to buy their houses or afford high rents by themselves. That's great for them, of course, but it ignores the evidence that, for most women on average salaries, it is very difficult, and often means spending a larger portion of your salary than is considered affordable.

Despite there being millions of single people living around the world, there is a frustrating gap in the statistics. The UK government's report on poverty, for example, includes different topics dedicated to the intersection between poverty and disability, poverty and race, and poverty and employment, but no chapter on the correlation between poverty and relationship status, which feels like a huge oversight and probably explains why ministers have been slow to factor single people into their policies. I've also been disappointed that no think tank, as far as I can discover, has researched outcomes for single people. Think tanks play an important role in influencing power and informing policy, but it apparently seems we single folk are not worthy of their attention. I'm disappointed, but not really surprised.

There are more stats available, however, when it comes to single parents and pensioners. Nearly half of children in lone-parent families live in poverty, compared with one in four of those in couple families. Of the working-age adults, lone parents are by far the most likely of any family type to be struggling with poverty. When we look at pensioners, the poverty rate for single pensioners is double that of couple pensioners, and almost one in five pensioners overall are living in poverty, according to the Joseph Rowntree Foundation.

Kylie Noble, a working-class writer who works in health and social care in Sheffield, knows only too well how difficult it can be to survive on one very low income. As a disabled person, who is also autistic, she found the house shares that are so common in your twenties really difficult to handle. In response, she moved from London to Doncaster after a period of poor mental health in early 2020, partly because it's cheaper to rent in the north.

She told me: "Flatmates would comment on how little I spoke, and I didn't really get the social rules. Since I got diagnosed, I've realized how much it helps me to live alone, but this is really hard when you're on such a low income." She says, "I've been claiming benefits for the last few years. It has made up a significant majority of my income, even though I have actually been working. There were some periods where the universal credit didn't cover all of my rent even, and I didn't know what to do. I honestly understood in those moments why people started selling drugs or turned to sex work."

Kylie, who is non-binary and uses both she/they pronouns, now lives in a tiny studio flat that she describes as more of a "retro bedsit" and "very cramped." There are other downsides too, and sometimes she wishes she had a romantic partner to support her and share the costs.

"It's hard, as when you're single and on benefits, you end up living in areas often described as 'rough'—with more crime and poverty. Like many disabled people, I also don't drive. And I think women who drive are so much safer, as they don't have to walk through dangerous places at night. Sometimes, when I'm traveling home and have to get off one bus and get on another bus and then walk up a really big hill, or I'm coming home late at night and am feeling unsafe, I think, 'Wouldn't it be nice if I had a partner who could just come and pick me up?' I usually have that thought only about twice a year, though."

Kylie says they are used to being left out of the conversation. "I grew up working class, from a very rural place, I'm queer, I'm non-binary, I'm disabled. I'm an Irish person living in England. I'm single and on benefits in a country that talks all the time about 'hardworking families.' But I've always been outside the conversation or on the margins and have always not really been factored in, so I'm just used to it by now. But in general I do find it hard to live in such a conservative country. It's been eye-opening for me."

Racism and Fatphobia

I wanted to speak to more people who feel like they are already on the margins, even before you factor in their relationship status. In 2020, Tola Doll Fisher wrote a guest piece for my newsletter about her experiences of being single and black. As she put it, even those who are not actively dating are impacted and most are very aware of how they will be perceived and treated if they do decide, for example, to get on the dating apps.

In the article, Tola, who I have also interviewed for a later chapter, wrote:

> Single, Black, Female. Now in my thirties, these three words are guaranteed to elicit sympathetic looks at best and a figurative and literal swipe left at worst. Did you know that, in 2014, dating website OkCupid ran a study that revealed black women received the fewest messages of all its users? Even if you are happily single and not looking to be in a relationship, there's something deeply unsettling about knowing that the majority of people in the dating pool would never even consider you.

> The year I was obsessed with *Love Island* was like playing a constant game of hide and seek with my TV. I couldn't bear to watch when the black girl was always, always picked last. The show that gave me the most feels this year was *Love Is Blind*, in which Lauren (black) and Cameron (white) met and fell in love before they had seen each other. I was ecstatic—and much relieved—that a positive representation of a black woman being loved had finally been shown on screen. But one couple among around eight billion people in the world does not enough of an example make.

For Stephanie Yeboah, the feeling of being unwanted seeped into every area of her life during her lengthy period being single. As well as being a black woman, she is also plus-sized, and experiences the added prejudice that often comes with that.

She told me: "I am so used to not being liked, or being found attractive or being seen as desirable. I just got used to that, and it got to the point where I realized I had allowed my lack of self worth to dictate so many things in my life, even with regards to my career."

There were so many things she wanted to do, but she stopped herself from even trying. "I didn't allow myself to go for those opportunities, because I thought that I was too big or I was going to be the only black one there or I was going to be different in some way," she said.

This began at a young age, when she dreamed of attending The BRIT School, a leading performing and creative arts school, which is based in Croydon. "I was around twelve or thirteen and I wanted to sing and was applying to do musical theater there, but I made my mum withdraw my application, because, when I'd gone to the auditions, I was the biggest one there and I had no self-belief in myself. This became a pattern for years, where I would drop out of things because I didn't think I'd be accepted."

This feeling got worse as she got older and her friends began to get asked out and started relationships. "I found myself constantly apologizing to people for my body. I started doing a lot of crash dieting, and it got to a point where I lost a lot of weight very quickly. Even though I was smaller, mental health-wise I was all over the place and I was very ill physically. That was the point where I knew it needed to stop, because I felt like I was slowly killing myself and who was that for? I realized I needed to learn to love myself and build my own self-esteem."

Stephanie is now in a relationship but found that people were surprised or even disappointed when she introduced her new boyfriend on social media, as they expected her to be single and remain that way, and to continue sharing her dating woes. This is something Stephanie explores more in a later chapter.

When Everyone Just Expects You to Be Single

When I interviewed Lucy Webster, a writer and the author of *The View from Down Here*, she brought up how often people assume and expect her to be single. There's this idea that she must be single because she uses a wheelchair.

"It annoys me when people think I'm single because I'm disabled or just expect me to be single. My extended family, for example, never questions me about my love life like they do with others. Although one time my cousin's new husband did and everyone freaked out and said, 'Why would you ask her that?'"

That isn't to say she hasn't faced prejudice when she has been on dating apps in the past, because she has. In 2021, she accidentally went viral on Twitter when she tweeted that a dating agency told her that finding someone would be challenging, because people would be put off by her wheelchair, essentially telling her that she was "too disabled" and so they wouldn't be able to help her find love.

She tells me: "Even without that experience, being a disabled person on dating apps is wildly horrible. It just makes you sad and I thought, 'What am I doing to myself and why?' It didn't seem worth it."

On the apps, she came across men who said they weren't interested and said they didn't want to end up having to look after her. There were also questions about whether she could even have sex.

"I decided to stop, and thought I would try again, but I haven't. As a disabled person, you're so conditioned to proving yourself worthy by doing what everyone else is doing that you don't really ask yourself if that's really what you want to do."

Lucy points out there is a difference between choosing to be single and being single because you have no choice. Contrary to what people probably think, it's still possible to be happy even if you fit into the latter category, but she says it is an important distinction.

"A lot of single positivity seems more for those who are single by choice, but when you haven't chosen it, that doesn't mean you have to be sad," she says. "There's just a difference between choosing it and not choosing it but feeling fine and happy with life anyway. I think that goes for any sort of minority. I have found the middle ground."

A few years ago I mentioned in a piece of writing that there was nothing wrong with you if you were single. I received a complaint, via email, from someone who thought I was being ableist. Some people, she wrote, do have things "wrong" with them and that is why they are single. She felt this about herself. A few months later, I wrote a newsletter about being diagnosed with ADHD. The same person contacted me again and said something along the lines of: "See, you are disabled too, so there is actually something wrong with you!" It came across as a total "gotcha" moment, like I'd been caught out for lying. The person in question went on to harass me so much I had to block her, so the whole experience was quite nasty, but I wondered whether she had a point.

I told Lucy about this encounter and asked what she thought. I only wish I'd had her answer at the tip of my tongue when I'd first received that email.

Lucy said: "Some people have a lot of internalized ableism. People assume that I believe I'm single because there is something wrong with me, but I actually think I'm single because there is something wrong with the world. If the world wasn't so ableist, it would be less likely that I was single."

She adds that she sympathizes with the person who wrote to me, because rewiring that ableism in yourself is hard. "The world tells you you're unlovable, and even though you realize that's crap by the age of twenty-five or so, you've already had all those years of thinking that way before you realize," she said.

Of course there are many more ways in which being single can be an extra layer of burden if you are already marginalized. And it can be hard not to feel angry when I listen to the stories of people like Kylie, Tola, Stephanie and Lucy, but things won't change unless we shine a light on them. Lucy's point about there being a difference between being single by choice and not is so important. I know some people reading this book will feel they don't have a choice, and I hope you know you're not alone.

THREE

One Is a Whole Number

"I'd rather be a free spinster and paddle
my own canoe."
—Louisa May Alcott

The year is 2019 and I'm in Italy again. It's my first time returning since I lived there for a summer after my breakup with James. I'm remembering how sad I was then. Things are so different now. I smile to myself, thinking how far I've come as I sunbathe stark naked on the bed of the apartment I'm staying in. The double doors to the Juliet balcony are open and the sun is blaring through, warming my bare skin. I'm feeling pretty smug about the fact I've worked out a way to sunbathe without leaving the house, and while I'm hoping none of the neighbors can see, part of me doesn't really care. I feel beautiful, confident, sexy, and joyful, even. And another thing? I'm completely and utterly alone. In a few hours, I'll take myself to the local bar and order myself a glass of the local wine—which, thanks to the tradition of aperitivo, comes with olives and crisps—and I'll sit there by myself, smiling like an idiot, thinking: this is la dolce vita.

Despite feeling so happy, there is a little thought that is running very quietly in the back of my mind. It's just whirring there in the background, niggling at me to pay attention. The thought is that some people find the idea of me being on my own on holiday quite sad. There are people who think I must be terribly lonely. They are wrong. And yet it still bothers me that some people seem to judge or pity me.

When I'd told friends and colleagues that I was planning this trip to the Italian countryside, to stay in a friend's empty flat by myself, they kept responding with, "Oh, if you'd told me, I would have taken some time off and gone with you." Those responses were sweet, but missed something crucial: being on my own was exactly what I wanted. Partly because I was striving to hold on to the younger version of myself who picked herself up after that first week in Italy and ended up having the most amazing summer, and then, later, moved to Spain all by herself. And partly because I was about to make a life-changing decision to go freelance, and potentially move back to my hometown, and needed some headspace to figure it out.

In the two years that followed my first Italian adventure, I worked hard on getting over James, fell head over heels for the guy who dumped me in the gastro pub, moved to Spain and then quite quickly got myself a Spanish boyfriend. After I broke up with him, the Spaniard, the following year—and then felt strangely sad when he got a new girlfriend—I moved back to the UK. Within six months, I had decided to stop dating and be single for a while. Thinking back now, I was in the middle of a huge transition. As well as leaving Spain, I had also left my career teaching English as a foreign language, which I had been doing for the previous three years in different countries. I had moved to London for the first time in order to retrain as a journalist. I was living and working in a boarding school in order to afford to be able to do an unpaid internship. I'd just been through the aforementioned period of back-to-back heartbreak. In this state of upheaval, I was questioning my life. I wondered what was wrong with me and why I was constantly treated badly and why no one loved me and generally feeling sorry for myself. It was at this low point that I came across two separate things that changed everything for me.

The first just sent a little shock wave while the second was a whole epiphany. Now, I know that people think the Myers-Briggs test is total bollocks, and it probably is, but I decided to give it a go, and one thing it said made me go "Oh." It told me that I am ENFP-T, otherwise known as The Campaigner, which wasn't at all a surprise, as it describes me perfectly. The part that caught my eye was about relationships and how people with this personality type tend to throw themselves into the first exciting part of a relationship, falling in love hard and quick, but struggle when it comes to commitment and the relationship settling down. In short, they thrive off the drama and excitement, but aren't as good at knuckling down to make a relationship actually work. I thought: "This rings a bell."

Shortly afterward, I watched a documentary by an Argentine filmmaker on the *New York Times* website. It was called *35 and Single* and it was probably the first thing I had come across that explored solo life, and the one that had the biggest impact on the way I view my life as a single person. After years of relationships and breakups, Paula Schargorodsky used the documentary to contemplate the role of love in her life and whether she needed to marry to find real happiness. She used the film to ask some questions that made me stop in my tracks. One of them was: "Can social mandates be disregarded, or is my extended youth finally coming to its end?"

In the film, she documented how while she continued to change boyfriends and hometowns every two years or so, her friends got boyfriends who became husbands and then got pregnant, until the footage shows the friendship group surrounded by children. (This is just like me, I thought.) Meanwhile, her traditional Jewish family couldn't understand why she wasn't following suit, telling her, essentially, that she needed to grow up. She goes on to say that while she moved around a lot, traveling for work, she was always looking for intense passionate love affairs and she found many. Each one, she said, was, she thought at the time, the love of her life. (Ding, ding, ding! Me too, I thought.) In the film she says she met Mr. Right, who her family all approved of, but when the time came to get married, she knew it wasn't what she actually wanted, so they broke up. I was twenty-nine when I watched it and had been living that exact kind of life, jumping from intense love affairs to new countries and jobs every couple of years. It was like looking into the future.

It was after watching this film, while thinking about what the personality test said, that I realized I wanted to take some time off and be single for a while. Although there had been situations where I was treated badly or been taken advantage of, I realized I wasn't a victim and that I had been choosing relationships that were only meant to burn for a short time, and then wondering why they weren't turning into a perfect relationship. I was actively choosing people who were never going to commit to me but pretending I wasn't. It was the ultimate moment of self-realization about what I'd been doing. I wasn't single because boys were mean and wouldn't love me back. I was single because I was, in fact, the commitment-phobe. (To paraphrase Taylor Swift, I was the problem.) This wasn't just about romantic relationships either. I was doing it in other areas, most notably my career, which I had a habit of totally changing every couple of years. I didn't want journalism and writing to be another flash in the pan. I wanted to choose a place to live and get embedded there instead of living the temporary existence I had been up until that moment.

There was more to it as well. The film ends with Paula saying: "Now I realize that everything I was looking for was much closer than I thought. Whether with someone or alone, those glimpses when you love and accept yourself totally, the world around you changes. In the end, happiness is a choice, isn't it?"

I mulled these sentences over and over in my head. I wouldn't have admitted it at the time, but they made me feel uncomfortable. The truth was that, as much as on the surface I could pretend I knew all of this, I didn't really know what she was talking about. I could talk about self-love, but I hadn't really embodied it. I didn't know whether I'd be able to find what I was looking for in myself. I wanted to love myself, but a cynical voice would rise up inside me and mock the very idea. But even though this part of the film felt like a mystery to me, I was deeply intrigued. I knew as soon as I finished watching the documentary that I wanted to learn how to love myself and stand on my own two feet instead of letting my self-worth hinge on what the next unsuitable guy I fell in love with thought. I also wanted to embrace the freedom that putting romance on the back burner would give me. I wanted to experience what would happen if I truly learned to accept myself. I desperately wanted to be able to nod in agreement when Paula asked the final question.

Happiness and Being Single Can Go Hand in Hand

In the years since I first watched Paula's documentary, I really have learned that happiness and being single can go hand in hand. For many people, though, this is something they simply cannot comprehend. For some it even makes them feel angry. At the Hay Festival in 2019, Paul Dolan, a professor of behavioral science at the London School of Economics, introduced his book *Happy Ever After*, which discusses happiness data surrounding relationships. So far, so unremarkable, you might think. Well, Paul thought so too. But after talking, and after his comments were written up by a *Guardian* journalist, he unexpectedly found himself at the center of a backlash, with people furious with him for daring to suggest what he had. And what were these extremely controversial findings? That the healthiest and happiest population subgroup are women who never married or had children. They weren't just happy; they were happier than those with spouses and children. That was the part that really seemed to rub people up the wrong way.

Paul replied in his own article, and wrote:

> My conclusion—that single women might be healthier and happier than married women and married women with children—was met with surprise from many, delight from single women and shock and even outrage from other quarters, especially on social media.
>
> Many pointed to their own experience to criticize me, saying that they—or their wives—were happier now that they were married or parents than they were when they were single. One man tweeted photos of his wife as apparent proof. I was accused of spreading propaganda. "How far will the media push this 'independent woman' narrative?" was one popular tweet.

Paul may have been ripped apart on social media, but there is actually robust evidence to back up what he said. One reason is to do with social connections. Single people are more likely to foster social connections that bring them fulfillment and they are also more likely to volunteer and to participate in social community events.

"Social connectedness is linked to happiness—so this might go a long way toward explaining why single people aren't as miserable as many people would imagine (and, it seems, sometimes even hope) them to be," Paul writes.

This certainly rings bells for me, for while I do enjoy solo holidays and even solo dates, I'm a people person and love nothing more than chatting to people, whether that be with friends or perfect strangers—and I like to get involved and take part. And in fact, shortly after sitting outside that bar in Italy on my own, I got chatting to the extremely cool bar staff and had a good laugh with them before meandering home. Being someone who is single, lives alone and is freelance, I spend an awful lot of time on my own, so, for me, carving out time in my week for "social connectedness" is something really important, whereas for others who can just stay in with their partner, they might not feel the need to get out there as much.

Single by Choice

Even though I know this, it's still so interesting to me that single women are supposedly the happiest group, according to some studies—and it's something that always raises eyebrows when I tell people, whether they are in relationships or not. When it comes to learning to stand on your own two feet and embracing single life, however long you are going to be single for, it can help to hear other stories, even if they are totally different to your own. One of the people I have featured in my newsletter is Mollie Quirk, a young woman in her mid-twenties, who has never had a boyfriend and is open about "still" being a virgin.

In a guest piece, she wrote that when she admits she has been single her whole life, people usually don't believe her and think it's "impossible, a myth, and something that surely can't be true." But she answers: "I guess I'm living proof. Living proof of basking in solitude and living a life that's truly authentic to myself and a life that's completely on my terms . . . even if society doesn't agree with me."

On what makes her happy to be single, she said:

> Not only do I do everything I want to do in my life free from judgment, but I've never had to rely on anybody to bring me joy or make me feel good about myself—I've only ever had to rely on myself. Whether it be hyping myself up and giving myself a confidence boost, or doing things that spark happiness in my day-to-day life.
>
> We're taught to conform to the notion that we all need somebody—a person that we live with, love with, and share our lives and ourselves with. But what if this isn't what we want?
>
> I've never been in a relationship, had a first kiss, had sex, and I've never had to factor somebody else's feelings and schedule into my life.

Single people, women especially, she says, are expected to find love and settle down before their mid- to late twenties—but this timeline isn't for everybody. "Life could be made easier by more people accepting that being single can be and is a choice," she adds.

Mollie was only twenty-five when I featured her, and it could be argued that, given she is so young, it's not a big deal that she has always been single (although given the reactions when she shares her story, I don't think that's true). What about the single people who have been single for decades?

Ketaki Chowkhani, who designed the first ever single studies course at postgraduate level in India, and maybe even the world, which she also teaches, has always been single. She grew up in a tiny, spiritual community in south India, which was founded by Aurobindo Ghose and Mirra Alfassa in the 1940s. In this community, marriage was actively discouraged by the leaders. This is because they believed marriage is bondage and therefore not compatible with striving for a spiritual life. The philosophy, instead, centered around the individual and the community, so individuals all had their own rooms, while everything else—eating, work, leisure, laundry—was done together as a community.

When Ketaki realized that there was a dearth of single role models for young people, she was able to draw on a rich legacy of single life from her own experience, which inspired the course. She told me that, despite her early years growing up in this community, she wasn't immune to the pressure to get married. She was aware of conversations about her cousins or her friends and when they would get married and who to.

"I was around fifteen or sixteen and I began to question the idea of marriage myself," she said. "Why is the only goal for a woman to get married and to be married to a particular kind of a person in a particular kind of a family? Why is that? Why is that the goal of a woman? I mean, we have so much more to do and give," she said.

When it came time for her family to find her a husband, she realized her standards were high—too high for the kinds of men put forward—and knew marriage wasn't for her. After this realization, she decided to choose a single life. Her parents accepted this, and she realized how much her upbringing in the spiritual community probably influenced her.

"For me, becoming single by choice was me claiming back that legacy of my childhood and claiming back that way of life where the focus is more on yourself and the community and spirituality rather than talking about marriage and family and social convention."

*

In the US, Bella DePaulo is a researcher in her seventies and has made it her life's work to study single people. She told me about how coming across the phrase "one is a whole number" in 1992 shifted her perspective and launched her interest in researching the psychology of living single.

She says: "I started this folder of thoughts. I collected

observations and clippings and things I saw in the media. The very first one was an advice column. The reader had written in to say she was so lonely. I think her spouse had just died and one of the things the advice columnist wrote in response was that 'one is a whole number' and so I underlined that and I put it in my file.

"It was kind of stunning to me that anyone would need to be reminded that one is a whole number, but of course they do because we have been so inundated with this messaging that we all need to have a romantic partner and, if we don't, we're incomplete."

Bella has continued to be single ever since, but it took her a while to realize that, for her, it wasn't a temporary state. She wrote: "I never needed to be personally reassured that one was a whole number as I loved being single, but what I didn't know and had to learn was that I always would love being single."

Realizing that loving being single was possible and fully embracing her single life, instead of sitting around waiting for someone to come along, was actually what made her happy. Like me, though, she doesn't love everything about her single life. One reason is that marriage offers people a special status in society, both in terms of status and things like tax breaks.

DePaulo had been sucked in by what the media and fairy tales tell us about marriage being the be-all and end-all too, and had assumed that science would confirm that married people are happier—but when she began to research, she realized it wasn't the case. Like Paul Dolan, she found that, when appropriate methodologies were used, single people were not actually more lonely or more depressed or more stressed than coupled-up people. This is despite the fact that single people aren't getting any of the caring and commitment from a spouse and their lives aren't celebrated the way married people's lives are, and that they also aren't getting any of those legal benefits, tax breaks and protections.

Since then, she has made it her mission to prove that untold numbers of people are what she calls "single at heart." She says: "People who are single at heart live their best, most fulfilling, meaningful, authentic and psychologically rich lives by remaining single. They are not single because they are unlucky in love or have had bad experiences or they never met the right person or that they have issues. They don't believe it's better to be single than in a bad relationship because that's too grudging. They know that, for them, it's just better to be single. Full stop. It's who they authentically are."

She says she wishes that people would understand that not having a serious romantic partner does not have to limit our lives. "In my experience and in my research, I have found that rather than limiting us, it throws our lives wide open. We are not the co-creators of our lives.

We are not the co-planners. We get to be the directors of our own lives. We can thrive this way."

I love everything these women have said, but, of course, not everyone is single by choice. What about those who have been through a painful breakup after being married for a long time? Have they been able to find happiness despite never imagining they would be single again and never wanting to be? I've never been married, and my longest relationship has been around four years (and it was when I was very young), so it's hard for me to imagine how difficult it would be to suddenly be single after more than two decades with someone.

When Being Single Isn't a Choice

Helen Thorn, one half of the Scummy Mummies, a comedy duo who aim to show motherhood in all its messy glory through their podcast and stand-up shows, showed me I was right to believe. Those who wouldn't otherwise have chosen to be single can also achieve happiness on their own. In fact, she's so passionate about this, she wrote a book with the title *Get Divorced, Be Happy.*

Helen, who is a mum of two, told me in an interview for my newsletter that she and her now ex-husband had been together for nearly twenty years, after getting together in their late teens. While acknowledging that she had missed out on dating in her twenties, her perception of single life before she was single herself was that there couldn't possibly be any positives, and that she "never wanted to be single."

When her husband cheated on her and left the family, however, she became single whether she wanted to or not, but she was surprised by what she discovered. She told me: "I'm actually so glad I was proven wrong, because I adore being a single mum and I adore being a single woman in her forties."

She put her initial preconceived notions down to her upbringing. The daughter of a vicar, she now realizes that the way single women were spoken about in the church had an impact. "It was always 'poor lonely Betty,' and there was this idea that somehow they weren't complete if they were single and how could they possibly be happy?"

Suddenly finding herself on her own and deciding to run with it meant she had to confront her own ideas about what it means to be single, and also what it means to be lonely. "I really smashed my own ideas," she said. "I realized I was incredibly lonely in my marriage. I felt rejection there, not rejection now."

To live life without that rejection was truly liberating for Helen. It's a joy to read in her book and observe on social media how everything—from her relationship with her children to her relationship with her own body—has improved since that day in March 2020, when her husband packed up a suitcase and moved out. She coped so much better than she thought she would and is rightly proud of doing it all herself, and even says she is a better parent since the split.

Even though I don't have children, as Helen does, I still get that sense of satisfaction when I do something particularly badass on my own. Those memories of how incapable I felt when I landed in Italy back in 2011 after leaving my ex sometimes surface when I try something new. They serve as a reminder of why I'd never want to be so reliant on and co-dependent with anyone again. And that goes for if or when I do enter a new relationship too, as I don't believe the two things are mutually exclusive.

Single Joy in Later Life

Even those who become single much later in life can embrace the "one is a whole number" attitude. I've spoken to a number of older women who told me in no uncertain terms that they still have a lot of life to live and intend to make the most of it, even in the face of everyone assuming all pensioners are socially isolated and sat on their own watching TV day after day. That's not to take away from those that are lonely, of course, but just to point out that sometimes this perspective is a stereotype.

Jax Hill-Wilson, who is in her late sixties, has been single on and off since 2002. She loves it because she enjoys the freedom to make decisions and plan her life according to her preferences and life plan, she told me in an interview for an article I wrote for *Positive News*. It also means she spends more time with her grown-up children.

"[Being single] is an opportunity for more discovery. Post fifty, you have another whole thirty years of living. It's a new life to enjoy. I choose to see this stage as another twenty-five years to enjoy and experiment, rather than visualize myself being a lonely old biddy," she said.

And her advice for anyone wanting to feel content about their single status? "Don't compare yourself to others in different situations; celebrate your choices as uniquely yours and see this is an opportunity for more discovery."

Jax is right. It really is an opportunity. Life goes on whether you have been single for five minutes, five years or fifty; we only have a short time on earth, so we shouldn't waste it sitting around waiting for someone else to come along and make us feel whole. We are whole already.

My Ten-Year Anniversary

While I was editing this book, I went to see Rebecca Lucy Taylor—better known as SELF ESTEEM—performing in Birmingham. I went to the gig with two other thirty-somethings, one I knew a little and one I didn't know at all. Perhaps because of the kind of vulnerable and honest music we were about to hear, our conversation skipped the small talk. Within ten minutes of meeting, we began exchanging war stories of times in our single and/or childless lives where we have been pushed to the side and seen as less important than our married friends with kids. Some of the things we didn't even need to say because it didn't need explaining. The story exchange continued in a frenzy of "Oh my God, I relate" and "That happened to me too," right up until the moment the lights went down and the performance began. By the end of the night we had our arms round each other, swaying and singing along to the music like we'd known each other forever.

The gig was a near spiritual experience for me. Aside from the music and the performance, it was how it felt to be united with thousands of others all being unapologetically ourselves at the same moment in time. It felt as if we were all worshipping in one of those evangelical churches where the congregation rejoice loudly and don't shy away from letting themselves go. Is it, I wonder, the fact that some of SELF ESTEEM's lyrics, which include thoughts on marriage and everyone having children, are the type of things lots of us secretly think but feel we shouldn't say out loud? And yet, in that room, we all felt safe and confident enough to chant them at the tops of our voices, in communion with each other. It felt liberating, empowering and all those other clichés. At times I felt like I was going to levitate.

Mid-show, I also realized something. It had been ten years that month since I last called someone my boyfriend. The thought made me laugh. It seemed to have crept up on me. "It's my tenth anniversary of being single," I thought, rolling the idea around my head. Instead of making me feel sad or embarrassed, I felt strangely proud of myself. Impressed, actually. It's like my younger self—that clingy, needy girl who would do anything for love—had stepped out of my body and was looking over in shock and awe that I'd actually managed it. "Fair play," she says. "I didn't think you had it in you."

The opening bars of "I Do This All the Time"—Rebecca's mission statement of sorts—began, and jolted me back to reality. As she told us not to be intimidated by all the babies others have had, tears filled my eyes. I thought: SELF ESTEEM gets it. These girls I'm with get it. Every soul in this room gets it. Isn't that the most powerful thing you can experience? Total empathy and solidarity and understanding. It felt like a sigh of relief, like a weight had temporarily lifted off my shoulders. I felt alive. I felt free—and the realization of how long I'd been single only added to this feeling of liberation and joy.

On the way back from the gig, still feeling high, I thought again of Paula Schargorodsky's documentary. I realized I could now nod along in agreement when she says that happiness is a choice. Even when things are crap, we can choose to look for the light. We can choose to make the most of our lives and can choose to appreciate and feel grateful for the good in our lives instead of focusing on what we're lacking. We can choose not to miss out on joy and how great it is to just be our authentic, true independent selves.

Even if you want to find someone tomorrow, I think that letting the fact that you can feel—and actually are—complete on your own really sink in could make your day today as a single person so much better. From my own experience, knowing that I'm not one half of a person gives me an inner confidence that is priceless. As Bella DePaulo points out, one really is a whole number.

FOUR

Where Is the Love?

> "To love well is the task in all meaningful relationships, not just romantic bonds."
>
> —bell hooks

A while ago, *The Guardian* published an article about women who are involuntarily celibate. It explored what it is like for women to go without a partner when they long for one—and how it feels when even a fleeting sexual connection feels impossible. At the time the piece was published, "incels" were the topic of much discussion. For those who don't know, "incel" is short for "involuntary celibate," and incels are members of an online subculture of men who define themselves as unable to get a romantic or sexual partner despite desiring one. The movement is fueled by misogyny and abuse of women. The journalist who wrote the *Guardian* piece wanted to explore the flip side and found women were more likely to blame themselves rather than anything external.

It was a moving piece and there were some great interviews. However, there was one aspect of the article that I found jarring, and that was the headline that was used for the print version: "The Women Who Live Without Love." The irony was that many of the interviewees in the article, while sad not to have a romantic partner, talked about community and friends and having active social lives. It got me thinking about where we give and receive love when we are on our own. I may not always have romantic love in my life, but that doesn't mean I live without love.

Thinking about this reminds me of a conversation I had at a party on a houseboat nearly a decade ago that really made me appreciate the love my friends and I have for each other. The party was in full flow. The music was loud. Some people were dancing. Others were having heated—and drunken—debates. A cluster of people hovered by the table of food and munched on crisps. But my friend Lizzie and I were not paying the slightest bit of attention. Instead, we were wrapped around each other on one of the sofas that was more like a bed. Our legs were intertwined and I was stroking her hair. She'd been having a tough time and I was holding her as she cried. We stayed like this for a while until she decided we should get drinks and join the party. As I sat up and my friend moved toward the kitchen, an older guy I'd never met before started speaking to me.

"I was watching you and your friend," he said.

"Oh," I said, shifting uncomfortably and wondering how to get away.

My concern must have shown on my face, because he hurriedly explained himself: "Not in a pervy way. I just thought it was beautiful and it also made me jealous."

I still wasn't sure where he was going with this, so I waited for him to continue.

"You know, women are able to really cuddle their friends. You can hold each other the way you were doing when you are sad—and men, for the most part, we just can't do that with our mates," he said, taking a sip from a beer bottle.

"I hadn't thought of it like that," I said.

"Yeah. It makes me wonder about male suicide. You know it's so high?" he asked, and I nodded. "I don't know, but maybe fewer men would kill themselves if they were able to really show how sad they are to their friends and let their friends hold them and cuddle them.

"Even when we have partners, we don't always want to show that side, show weakness or whatever. And of course plenty of men are on their own," he said, making air quotes when he said the word "weakness."

He went on to tell me about some difficult moments in his

life, and how disconnected he felt from his male friends, who struggled to know how to handle his pain.

That conversation had a huge impact on me. I didn't realize until that moment how lucky I was to have the kind of relationships with my friends where I can have a lingering cuddle or hold their hands or stroke their hair. It kind of broke my heart to look into this guy's eyes and realize that men—most, but not all—can't get that kind of platonic comfort. I never saw him again and I didn't catch his name, but I think of him every single time I see female friends being tactile with each other, and I also think of it every time a male friend is having a hard time. They deserve to have their hair stroked by their best friend too.

I honestly believe one way to dismantle the patriarchy would be to take away the stigma—and intrinsic homophobia—that stops men from getting comfort and love outside of sexual contact. Maybe there would also be fewer incels in this world.

The thing is, my friends are the loves of my life. Some of the best moments in my life have happened in the company of friends—and they've been the ones who have helped me through some of the worst moments of my life. Perhaps controversially, I actually think they are just as important as family—though I'm lucky enough to get a lot of love from my family too. I love making friends. I love that delicious feeling when you first meet someone and just know they are going to be an important part of your life. I love falling in love with new friends. Being an extrovert, who thrives on social connections, I'm fortunate to have lots of friends. I've collected them over time and, in much the same way as how I feel about my overly large book collection, I'm often reluctant to let them go—even when they hurt me or I hurt them. Sometimes friends will even mock me for how many best friends I have, when I say things like "my best friend from school" or "my best friend from uni" or "my best friend from when I lived in Spain."

Receiving Love

Even so, sometimes I can forget how lucky I am to be surrounded by love. One instance that stands out is my thirty-first birthday. Turning thirty had been truly joyful; as well as feeling relieved I'd survived my tumultuous twenties, I also had a wonderful time celebrating with my loved ones. But, the following year, I was feeling really low about where I was in my life. I was subletting the small cramped room in the council flat, trying and failing miserably to land a contract at my dream publication, and was unhappy about being single. I just felt like nothing was going right for me. I cried to a friend, who is a little older than me and had been long-term single herself, about having to wake up on my own on my birthday.

On this particular birthday, several of my best friends couldn't make it due to holidays and illnesses. Only a small mix of friends from different friendship groups were going to be coming. I was fretting about trying to please everyone and couldn't decide what to do. In the end, I decided on a Sunday roast at my favorite pub, followed by a walk on Hampstead Heath. I wasn't really looking forward to it, though, and was worried others would find it boring.

I headed down before everyone else to decorate the table at the pub with silly photo booth props when I had a thought: "Shit, I forgot to buy a birthday cake." And then immediately: "That's the type of thing people buy for their partners on their birthdays." A lump rose in my throat, and I could feel tears starting to come. In hindsight, I must have had a temporary case of amnesia, because none of my ex-boyfriends had ever thought to buy me a birthday cake on my birthday, but I felt that loss hugely in the moment anyway. How nice it would have been for someone else to organize this meal and to treat me with a nice birthday cake. Why must I always do everything myself, I thought.

Out of the corner of my eye I could see some of my friends arriving, so I shook these feelings off and plastered a smile on my face. I wondered if anyone could tell how much I was faking being happy. One of the last to arrive was my cousin Lily. She was holding a box in her hands.

It wasn't until she got closer that I realized what it was. It was a birthday cake. She was in the middle of apologizing that it was just a shop-bought one when I threw my arms around her and buried my face in her shoulder. Tears once again sprang to my eyes. "Hey," she said, leading me aside. "What's all this about?" I explained and she gave me another hug and said, "That's what I'm here for, silly." It was such a little thing but it meant everything.

In the end, the day was perfect. Everyone got on much better than I thought. I remember looking round the table and feeling so grateful. The weather was beautiful for the walk and the Heath was looking its absolute best. I asked a stranger to take a photo of us all lined up, squinting in the October sun with the London skyline behind us. That photo makes me smile whenever it pops up on my Facebook memories, as it reminds me that being surrounded by friends and family is a wonderful thing—and that we should always take time to celebrate our birthdays even if we aren't really feeling it. There is no guarantee that we'll reach the next one, after all. In the words of my friend Tiffany Philippou, to celebrate birthdays is to celebrate life.

It isn't only during birthdays or difficult times when I really feel the love, though. I feel it every time I go to my parents' house on Sundays and, after being bombarded with licks by their dog Ruby, we enjoy a roast dinner together. I feel it every time a friend asks if I want to be picked up so we can go to the supermarket or an out-of-town retail park, which, as I don't drive, is always so thoughtful. I feel it every time my sister sends me an article I may have missed about single life, or sends photos of Ruby, because she knows I miss her. I feel it every time my parents come to help me with something in my house or at my allotment. I feel it whenever my best mate's daughter draws me a picture or sends me a video message. I feel it every time someone sends me something in the post, whether that's a gift "just because" or a letter or postcard. I feel it every time someone sends me a meme or reel that they know I'll find funny. I feel it every time I'm ill and my friends and family ask if I need anything from the shop. I feel it every time someone reads my newsletter and shares it on social media, even if they aren't single themselves. I feel it every time my cats snuggle up and relax into me.

Giving Love

Being on the receiving end of acts of love is great, but giving love can be just as fulfilling. Maybe because I find organizing my own parties so stressful, I'm also usually the one to help organize people's hen dos and baby showers, because I want to remove that stress for them. When Gemma, my best mate from school, got engaged, I was living in South Korea and was devastated not to be with her while she planned the wedding. So, instead, I asked my mum if she would make the bridesmaids' dresses, and, along with our friend Steph, I organized the hen do even though I was thousands of miles away. I had so much fun researching Dublin nightlife—and the weekend almost went off without a hitch. In fact, the only downside was when I managed to open a taxi door in Gemma's face—just four days before the wedding, necessitating a lot of makeup to cover the bruising—but even that has gone down in history and is now Gemma's favorite story to tell about her wedding.

When my friends are having a hard time, I'm usually the one to organize care packages, which I generally put together myself. I love choosing all the items and putting them all in a box to send off. I also love making presents, especially for special occasions. When my friend was getting married and feeling quite stressed, I ordered a vintage handkerchief from the internet and taught myself how to embroider, in a cursive font, onto it: "Keep your shit together, Louise." I chose blue thread, so as well as being her "something old," it was also her "something blue." While this may sound like a bit of a harsh thing to say, I knew she'd find it funny. It was a true labor of love. As I knew she would, she burst out laughing when she opened the gift. She made it her mantra on the big day and tucked it into her bra so that she'd have it close to her throughout. Afterward, she got it framed. Whenever I've been round her house since her wedding and seen my creation, I've had the same warm fuzzy feeling that I had the whole time I was making it—and that feeling is love.

When Friends and Family Are Your Real Soulmates

Writer and campaigner Poorna Bell has thought a lot about different kinds of love following the death of her husband, Rob, who took his own life in 2015. When she was younger, she loved the idea of meeting her one true soulmate. And though she had that with Rob, she has since realized that people can have more than one soulmate. That, in fact, friends and family can be soulmates too. She still counts Rob as a soulmate, but has come to realize that her sister Priya and her friend Mal are also her soulmates.

In an interview with me, she pointed out that nowhere in Maslow's Hierarchy of Needs (i.e., the five levels of the hierarchy: physiological, safety, love/belonging, esteem and self-actualization) is romance specifically mentioned. Instead, what's mentioned is a broader sense of love—and that can include love from friends, family, and even co-workers.

She tells me: "There's this construct that romantic love is the most important kind of love and I just don't believe that it is. I still don't think you can get everything that you need from one type of love. I think that it's really important to have a mixture of different types.

"I've been taught my entire life, through all the messaging we receive, that the goal was to find a romantic relationship and I think that what that meant was I didn't really value how important friendships and family relationships were and are. I don't mean to say that I discarded them or anything, but if I'd looked at a hierarchy of my relationships, I never really thought that they were on par. They always seemed to sit below, and so I think that, after losing Rob and after working out what that recalibration of my life was going to look like, I looked around and knew I needed relationships that really nourished me and that really looked after me."

Poorna says it wasn't that she didn't think you could have it within romantic relationships, but just that she realized how much she already had it within existing platonic relationships. "That kind of slow and steady love is what I want in my life. Very often, with romantic love, it's been the thing that's caused the most amount of pain in my life and it's let me down a lot. Consistency is the foundation of love and that's what I get with my loved ones."

At the time of writing, Poorna has been dating a guy for a while, but told me she didn't want to tell him about her upcoming birthday because she just didn't need an elaborate birthday planned by a romantic partner.

"I just don't have that need or expectation now for someone to prove themselves in that way and I don't need that validation. When it comes to really important and significant moments, such as sharing some amazing work news, I want to share that with the people who have consistently loved me and who are not just people that I love too, but the ones who've earned it, to hear about my life as well.

"Once you recognize who those people are in your life, I think it just allows you to value and give to them in a way that you just may not have really done before."

Community Love

While there is no denying that close friends and family are important, studies have shown that the loose connections we all have in our lives are also essential to our well-being. Think of the friendly barista at the coffee shop near your office, or the neighbor whose dog you always stop to pet when you see them in the park, or the woman who goes to the same yoga class as you. You might stop to have a little chat and exchange pleasantries whenever you see them, but you don't know them well. The sociologist Mark Granovetter calls these low-stakes relationships "weak ties." Although the word "weak" seems to signify that these kinds of connections wouldn't be that important, research published by Harvard in 2022 showed that those who interacted with a diverse "social portfolio"—including plenty of these weak ties—reported greater life satisfaction and higher levels of well-being.

This certainly rings true for me. I'm quite a chatty person and I love to meet new people. I remember finding it quite difficult when I first moved to London from Spain. In London people tend to avoid chatting to strangers, particularly on public transport, whereas in Spain I was always having little chats with strangers. This is also why I found the pandemic—when we were told to actively avoid others, especially strangers—particularly hard.

The pandemic was also what led Tola Doll Fisher to make the move from London, where she had lived her whole life but felt "unhappily invisible," to Cheltenham. In a guest piece for my newsletter, she wrote: "Many people couldn't wait to get back to 'normal life' during the infrequent lifting of restrictions, but all it did was highlight for me how lonely I was when things were 'normal.' My ex-husband and I lost our baby in 2012 and I was divorced in 2014. However, despite coming to terms with both those things, I still felt the isolation keenly observed by those who don't fit into society's couple- and family-oriented setup."

Moving to a town meant everything was local and the opportunities to build connections and become embedded in a community were far greater than in London, which can feel like quite an anonymous place to live.

"Every time I leave my house [here], I bump into someone I know and this sense of being seen and known is something I realize I need as a single person at this stage in my life," she said.

I've had a similar experience since moving back to Shrewsbury, though that's not to say you can't foster community in big cities. I have just made much more of an effort up here, perhaps fueled by the fact I've often written about social isolation in my journalism work.

The thing about building up positive relationships with neighbors and other people you frequently come into contact with, such as the person who often serves you in your favorite café, is that it can take time. But if you persevere, it can make all the difference to know there are people nearby who know you. I also try to be helpful as a way to connect. My former neighbors had both kids and cats. I knew they didn't live near family, so I told them if they ever needed a babysitter or someone to look after the cats while they were away, I would be happy to. They eventually took me up on it, I'm glad to say. I also attended a few community meetings about a local issue and helped where I could. This has meant I always have someone to say hello to in the street, as we recognize each other from those meetings. Getting an allotment also helped me, as many of the other allotmenteers are people who live in the streets surrounding mine.

Recently I've bumped into a cool couple who live a few doors down from me at the pub and at a friend's birthday party, which has really helped cement our slowly burgeoning friendship. Becoming a regular of a nearby coffee shop has also been important. I've begun conversations with those who work there, some of whom I now count as friends, and also I now recognize and can say hello to some of the other clientele. Getting to know people in my local area really helped make me feel more at home, less alone and part of the community.

Other Kinds of Love

Writer and disability advocate Lucy Webster has recently sworn off dating apps after a number of bad experiences, but says that she doesn't often get lonely, thanks to the support not only from her friends and family but also from her carers.

Due to the nature of her disability, she requires twenty-four-hour care, and she is on a mission to change people's perspectives, as many seem to believe that needing round-the-clock care must be awful and a tragedy.

For *The Guardian*, she wrote:

> Many fail to see the possibilities that care creates—not to mention the friendships that flourish within the care relationship. My PAs, past and present, are some of

> my best friends—but even this sentiment can give rise to unwanted sympathies. People assume it means I can't make friends elsewhere (for the record: also not true). My PAs are my friends not because they have to be but because we like each other. And because the bonds of trust, understanding and a shared lived experience are incredibly strong; often, they are the only ones who really see the effect inaccessibility and ableism have on my life.

Other people feel love thanks to being religious. Charlie Craggs, an award-winning activist, actress and author of *To My Trans Sisters*, is Catholic and says that feeling the love of God helps her through tough moments. One of the hardest times in her life was when her best friend, Khadija Saye, was killed in the Grenfell Tower disaster in 2017. Khadija, an artist who was just beginning to make her mark on the world, died aged just twenty-four in the fire, along with her mother and seventy others. Charlie's world fell apart. She and Khadija had been best friends since nursery school and had grown up in council estates in the same deprived area of London. They were both on the brink of making their career dreams a reality.

"It's hard to put into words how much it still hurts not to have her. Khadija was my number one," Charlie says. "I believe you can have platonic soulmates and that's what we were. No one in this world got me more than her. Not having a boyfriend was fine because I had her. When she went, I felt so alone and, in a way, I still do, because even though I have a lot of friends, I don't have anyone I was as close to as her. I have no one in my life now who I consider number one. I don't even have a number two. I just have a lot of number threes, fours, fives, etc."

While her other friends tried to be there for her, it was her belief in God and God's love that got her through. She says: "I feel lucky to be spiritual. Being a religious person has given me something to believe in when I'm feeling lonely. I'm really lucky that I've got that. I can always remind myself that there's a bigger picture and a bigger plan for me. I feel like one of the blessings of religion is that you can put all that in someone else's hands. That's how I get through those awful moments of loneliness, by remembering I'm not actually alone."

Loving Ourselves

As well as love from external sources, there is also the love we have for ourselves. Now I'm not advocating for some kind of toxic positivity bullshit here. I know it is hard to really love yourself 100% every single day. How we feel about ourselves—just as how we feel about others—naturally fluctuates.

Obviously this is something people in relationships can also practice and certainly isn't something we just need to do because we are single. We are not single because we need to improve ourselves. But I do appreciate how my love for myself has grown in the last decade and how much that has helped me feel more strong and stable. Sometimes people in relationships will describe their partner as being their rock and I can understand that, especially if they have been through a difficult time. But I have had to be my own rock, and that is why I am proud to say I love myself.

The term "self-love" is certainly not something I was ever taught at school or growing up. There is real stigma attached to it. Being told "you love yourself" is often an insult meant to imply you have a big ego or you're getting too big for your boots, so to actively and vocally decide to be the love of your own life is a bit rebellious. There is also the cringieness that many people have for anything that comes across as "woo-woo." Personally, I embrace it, but each to their own.

For Radhika Sanghani, it was a broken heart that led her to really think about and embrace self-love. It was important, because she could no longer rely on someone else to make her feel loved and worthy. She had actually been the one to break up with her boyfriend, after realizing it wasn't going to work long-term. Nevertheless, it was a heartbreaking decision. Around the same time, she left her staff job and went freelance.

"I knew I had made the right choices but, all of a sudden,

I lost a lot of things that gave me stability and also validation," she says. "So I had to start giving that to myself instead. I found it really hard in the beginning. I don't think we are taught to advocate for ourselves and embrace our self-worth when growing up."

What happened next would later inspire her novel *30 Things I Love About Myself*, she told me. She and her ex did the classic swapping of belongings that so often follows a breakup and, when she later opened the box of her belongings, there was a book inside that she'd never seen before. His flatmate had thought it was hers, so he chucked it in, but to Radhika, it felt like a sign.

"The title of this book was literally *How to Love Yourself (and Sometimes Other People)* and it was a spiritual self-help book about self-love that was written by a Buddhist monk and a Christian woman. When I first started reading it, I thought it was weird, but the more I kept reading it on the train, I realized it was a gift," she says. "Spirituality is important to me and I just felt like that is actually part of my self-love. The two go hand in hand for me. Over the years, I have just deepened both of them."

Radhika says the book made her really question whether she loved herself. And so she made a conscious decision to work on it. At twenty-one, she'd written a list of things she loved about herself on a trip to New York while drinking a martini and channeling Carrie Bradshaw.

After reading the book, she decided to revisit the list and make a new one, which included deeper things than the one she had written in her early twenties (which had included things like that she loved her hair).

“Once I started on this path, I really began to notice my inner critic and how loud it was. I was having these negative thoughts all the time and, after a while, I was able to change those thoughts to more loving ones. I now refuse to criticize myself. I might occasionally do it out of habit, but I no longer actively do it.”

It was during this period that she became an influential body-positive campaigner and founded #SideProfileSelfie, a movement to celebrate big noses, which has reached millions—something, after years of hating her nose, she never would have believed she would want to do. Of course, sometimes external things would crop up, such as a rejection or a failure, and the insecurities would resurface and it was harder to think loving thoughts, but she says “the little kernel of self-love I started with has just got bigger and bigger.”

“Now, when something bad happens, I can draw on that,” she says. “It’s always there now, saying ‘But you’re great, remember, and we love you.’”

Radhika also keeps a photo of herself as a child by her bed, which helps remind her to be kind to herself. “I look at her and I have so much love for her, which is so easy because she's so cute. My love for her is so pure, but when I look in the mirror, it's more complicated. So I just try to aim for the sorts of feelings I have for little me. For me the way I express my self-love, is in how I treat myself and the way I talk to myself. I guess it's about being more mindful of myself and what's best for me."

All this work really helped her during a more recent breakup with the man she thought she was going to marry. The relationship's breakdown came out of the blue and really floored her. Yet, she noticed she recovered faster and her self-worth didn't take a beating, whereas in the past she would have felt worse, as she would also have been ruminating on all the things she might have done wrong or the ways in which she wasn't good enough.

Doing the (Self) Work

I really related to what Radhika said. A few years ago, not long after that relationship coach told me she thought I was traumatized, I threw myself into the world of "self-work." I did everything from hypnotherapy sessions to weekend courses. I bought self-help books, watched TED talks and listened to podcasts about living life (Cheryl Strayed's *Dear Sugar* was, and still is, my absolute fave). I completed The Artist's Way. I journaled and wrote out positive affirmations. I did countless yoga and meditation workshops. I started therapy. I even had a private

Instagram account, where I shared what I had learned alongside whimsical images. After a while I became totally exhausted from all the epiphanies and all the self-discoveries, so I decided to have a break from such active self-improvement and, looking back now, I realize part of what was motivating me was that I wasn't very happy and so I was trying to throw everything I could find at the problem. Some things were a lot more useful than others. However, despite my mixed feelings about the wellness movement, I'm still glad I went through this period, because I learned so much about myself. And a few things have stuck with me from that period. My approach to self-love is one of them.

During one workshop I attended, we were encouraged to actually say "I love you" to ourselves as often as possible. I remember the teacher suggesting we look in the mirror and say it out loud and keep saying it until it stopped feeling silly and you actually meant it. I went home and tried it when my flatmate was out. I repeated "I love you" over and over while looking myself in the eye until I realized I was crying. Not just crying. Sobbing. I had not expected that level of emotion. I think one of the reasons was I had a hard time believing I was worthy of those three magic words from anyone, let alone myself. It was a moment I won't forget. After that, whenever I went to the loo, I would mouth "I love you" at the mirror. I did this for ages, and even did it while using public loos when no one was paying attention. It gave me a little boost as I prepared to go back out and face the world.

To this day, I still finish all my journal entries with the words "I love you." Those three words really do hold a power and I genuinely do believe myself now. I have an occasional agony aunt column, and someone once asked me about self-love. They were confused about how to go about it. After all, this isn't something we are generally taught in childhood (but should be!). If you are in the same boat, may I suggest you begin with the activity in the mirror? I know it sounds a bit barmy, and you might be cringing just thinking about it, but give it a go.

Find a mirror. Take a deep breath. Look yourself in the eye and say those three little words: I love you. Say it again. And again. Say it until you really mean it.

Once you have done that, you could choose to do something for yourself that feels special. A little treat, perhaps. Something that feels indulgent. As I'm writing these words, I'm staying in a nice hotel for the night. Somehow I was given an upgrade on arrival and so I have a superking-size bed all to myself. I'm going to order room service and put on a film. Perfection.

Something I have come to realize is that when we focus our energies on what we are lacking in life, it can make those things seem bigger in our heads and diminish the things we do have, so we believe they are less important.

When you take the love I have for myself and add in the love I get from my friends and family, I really don't think anyone could argue that I'm a woman who lives without love.

Solo Date Ideas

I asked members of my newsletter for ideas on where to go for a solo date. Here are their suggestions:

Go and watch a film at the cinema. Of all the places to go, the cinema is probably the least challenging for anyone who is new to doing things on their own. It's dark, nobody is allowed to talk anyway, and you can choose your seat in advance so there are no awkward conversations. The theater is another good option.

Go to an art gallery or museum. You can meander to your heart's content and stop at something you like for as long as you like without having to factor in someone else's interests and tastes. Also, lots of people go to galleries or museums alone, so you won't stick out.

Take yourself out for a meal. If you're nervous to go to a restaurant for an evening meal, start with going out for a nice lunch or breakfast. I always take my phone and book with me, but end up not picking up either as I spend the whole meal partaking in my favorite activity, which is people-watching. I also find that I focus more on the food and drink in front of me than I do when out with friends or family.

Book a massage in. It's such a great solo treat for anyone. Or you could take it further and go to the spa for the day. I did this on my thirty-seventh birthday and it was great. I enjoyed the gym, pool and sauna, etc. and then had a facial and a massage. I also had lunch. My birthday was midweek and it was so nice to mark the day doing something quite decadent.

Go to a new coffee shop with your journal or planner and take some time to think about your goals and what you want from life. Or if you're feeling creative, you could make notes about what you observe. There is a really nice mindful activity I do sometimes, where you jot down five things you can see, four things you can touch, three things you can hear, two things you can smell and one thing you can taste.

Go to a gig solo. The best thing about a gig, especially if you have a standing ticket, is that you can move around if anyone is bothering you. I have really enjoyed the gigs I've gone to alone as I can really let go and enjoy myself without having to match the mood and behavior of my friend, which I have the tendency to do.

A long walk in nature. I love walks with friends but sometimes I spend so much time chatting to them that

I don't pay much attention to what's around me. When you go alone, you really notice the sights and sounds. Make sure you text someone where you're going and when you should get back though, just in case you have a fall or something.

FIVE
Defying the Narrative

I've always been a big romantic. When I was a little girl, I loved fairy tales and Disney films and stories that ended with ". . . and they all lived happily ever after."

When I was six, I—along with my sister and another cousin—was asked to be a bridesmaid for my cousin Suzanne. The night before the wedding my gran and mum curled our hair with rags. We wore pink candy-stripe satin dresses that my mum, a talented dressmaker, had made. We had hoops and netting under our skirts. We had pink lace gloves and ballet slippers and carried our own little bouquets. We looked like little sugar-plum fairies as we eagerly waited outside the church for Suzanne. I couldn't believe my eyes when she arrived by horse and carriage—it was a proper eighties wedding, heavily inspired by Diana Spencer's wedding to Prince Charles. As Suzanne was helped down from the carriage, I remember thinking she looked like an actual princess. It was one of the most magical moments of my childhood.

From that moment on, I imagined my own wedding day would be similar. I don't remember ever doubting, when I was young, that I would one day get married and have a house and babies, just like my parents and all my friends' parents and just like all the main characters in the stories I read and watched.

Most of the stories we grow up with—from myths to fairy tales to Shakespearean plays and more—end with either marriage or death. The happy ending is marriage, the tragic ending is death. Those are generally the only two options available to any given female protagonist in a story. These stories perpetuate the idea that, to be happy, we all just have to find our one true love. The story usually goes something like this: the woman is on her own (either in danger or just miserable), then she meets a man—it's always a man because the stories are always about heterosexual relationships—who rescues her from the horror of being single, marries her in a big white wedding and then, of course, they all live happily ever after.

It's no wonder you feel like a failure when you find yourself single and in your thirties when all our cultural touchstones make you feel like a total freak of nature. Disney films don't show what happens after Cinderella kissed her prince and had to adjust to palace life, or

Jasmine struggling to get pregnant and having to go through IVF. We didn't watch *Sleeping Beauty* realizing that, actually, she fancies girls, not the bloke who just kissed her without her permission, or Ariel realizing that actually she felt unfulfilled with her new husband on dry land and would rather be single and back in the ocean.

Contrary to how this may sound, I'm not actually anti-romance. I'm quite the opposite. I still find weddings magical and I still cry at romantic comedies, and I even still enjoy Disney films. But I think one of the reasons the single stigma prevails is because of these stories we're told as children—and continue to be told as adults, through books, TV, films and by the media. Everything just seems to hammer home the point that being single is an anomaly. The characters who stay single also often end up being the butt of the joke.

Things are getting better, but slowly. In the 2013 Disney film *Frozen*, it's not romantic love that saves the day but sisterly love—and the protagonist, Elsa, remains single at the end of the film. The film's co-writer and co-director, Jennifer Lee, who was raised by a single and "very independent" mum, told *The New York Times* she isn't interested in any more Prince Charming characters who simply look good and show up at the right time.

Mel Johnson, the founder of The Stork and I, a community for solo mums by choice, has a daughter in infant school and is hyper aware of the impact that the stories her daughter Daisy hears may have on her and how she views the world. Daisy has story books about different kinds of families, but she also loves Disney films.

"Daisy is obsessed with *Cinderella*," Mel says. "She has watched one version, starring Camila Cabello, thousands of times. It came out recently and got a lot of stick in the press, but I actually love it. I thought the messaging in it was really good. Basically she says to the prince, 'I really like you, but I want to put my career first, so I'm going to have to do that,' and then he ends up following her around. Daisy loves it. Yes, she does fall in love, but it's a good message for her to say 'Even though I love you, this isn't going to work,' and then he is the one to drop everything for her. It's a complete role-reversal."

Daisy also loves Elsa. "I don't think it's quite dawned on her yet that Elsa doesn't have a love interest like almost every other Disney princess, but maybe that's a good thing that it's just subliminal," Mel says.

For our generation, there can be work to do, because we grew up with very traditional stories. Mel says it's been the conversations she's had and books she has read in recent years that have helped her change her own internal narrative about being single. For a long time she didn't think she had been influenced by societal pressures and the stories around what is normal and what is deemed successful, until she began to read more on the topic of singleness.

"When I first became known for being a solo mum, I went on a podcast and was asked whether I felt social pressure to become a mum, and I said, 'No, not at all. It wasn't anything to do with society. It was my own biological pressure.' Now I cannot believe I said that," she says.

"The penny finally dropped a few years ago, and it was thanks to everything I had been reading," she says. "I thought about how, in life, the biggest achievement we can have as women is to be given away at the altar. It's crazy when you really stop and think about it. We're so conditioned that success means marriage and that conditioning is backed up by the stories we hear and the way the world is designed for couples."

The Shame of Falling Outside the Narrative

It's not just in fiction where we encounter the issue. Every single day we all tell stories about ourselves and the world around us. When I started thinking more about the way society is designed for couples, I started to notice the ways in which the stories we consume and tell each other on a daily basis are often centered on relationships, marriage and babies. When we meet our friends and family, we tell stories from our week or stories we have heard from others. Perhaps we tell the story of someone's engagement or that someone else is pregnant. Even though I know this, I am still as guilty as the next person.

This feeds into attitudes toward being single. Anyone who has been single for a while will have a story about a time when they were judged or shamed for being single—from people asking, "How on earth are you still single?" (with the implication being that there must be something wrong with you) or people making "jokes," such as the time when I was having a difficult conversation with someone who asked, out of nowhere, if I was married. When I said I wasn't, he replied in a very self-satisfied and mocking way: "Didn't think so."

Sometimes the shame actually comes from other single people. A few years ago, I met an old work acquaintance of mine for coffee and told her that I was writing about being the only single one in my friendship group. I was met with silence. She looked at me, horrified, and finally said: "I could never talk about being single. I just wouldn't want to admit that . . . Like, don't you care that your ex-boyfriends might read it? I would never want mine to know I'm still single."

It's not always other people, though. Sometimes I'm the one shaming myself. Back when I was a full-time journalist, I was having an exciting months-long flirtation with someone I had seriously good chemistry with. While I was comfortable being open and even vulnerable with him, I was very careful never to mention when I last had a boyfriend. I kept things vague. I didn't want him to think there was something wrong with me. I feared it would change his opinion of me if he knew I'd been single for years. But it wasn't just with potential love interests. I felt awkward telling anyone. It felt almost like I was trying to do a PR job on my own life and brush what felt like the ugly truth under the carpet.

*

The stories we as a society tell each other about relationships or lack thereof don't just impact how we feel about being single—they also impact how we're expected to act, speak, look and behave.

I spoke to actor and playwright Rebecca Humphries, author of the memoir *Why Did You Stay?*, which explores how she escaped a toxic relationship, about the stories we are told and the stories we continue to tell ourselves about how women should act and what they should accept in romantic relationships. For a long time, she knew her relationship wasn't healthy, but it took a very public case of cheating—when her ex, the comedian Seann Walsh, was pictured kissing his dance partner from *Strictly Come Dancing*—for her to finally leave him.

She said: "There are so many stories where the woman is made to feel lucky that someone loves them, and that's certainly found its way into my psyche. I felt so lucky to be loved in whatever capacity. I got taught more as a child about how important it was to be in a romantic relationship and absolutely nothing about self worth."

Rebecca says millennial women are the last generation to really be taught those things and to get those messages from a really young age. "Now we're in this position where we're grown up and we know full well, because we're smart, intelligent, curious women, that all of that stuff is bullshit. But we've still got to do that unpacking at the same time, because it's so ingrained in us. We can intellectually know something is toxic but still think 'Oh, maybe if I stay, things will get better and he will love me.'"

Yes, She's Still Single, but Don't Worry: She Has a Career!

A few years ago, an older female relative was telling me a story about a woman she knows who, after a long period of being single, met someone and had a baby. I think she was telling me this story as her way of reassuring me that it could happen to me too. During this conversation, she made a comment about the woman being single for so long because she was "obsessed with her career." The words "like you" hung in the air between us, although she didn't actually voice them.

Being called a "career woman" is actually my biggest pet hate. Aside from it being a completely meaningless label, it's also inherently misogynistic. We do not call men "career men." It's often women who say this about other women, and it always feels very judgmental. It goes hand in hand with the way some people also view ambitious women in a negative light, which itself harks back to childhood, when little girls are called "bossy," while little boys are said to have "strong leadership skills."

I haven't just heard this from older family members. I've also been described this way by peers and even close friends. There was the time when I was trying to reassure someone who was newly single that things weren't so bad. A friend, on hearing me say in a joking and self-deprecating way that "it could be worse, she could be me," as I'd been single for so long and at that point wasn't happy about it, said: "Oh, but you've only been single so long because you've been focused on your career." Not long after, another friend told me about how her husband had described me as a "career girl." She seemed to think I would find this description absolutely charming.

The thing is that there are plenty of people who are "obsessed" with their career who are also in successful relationships or marriages and who have children. I know, because I've worked for a lot of them. It feels a bit like people are suggesting you can only have a career or a relationship and not both, like we have stepped back to the 1950s. I consider how focused I am on my job to be at a normal healthy level.

I have friends in all kinds of jobs who are just as ambitious as me and yet, because they have husbands and children, they aren't labeled as "career women" as much as I am, which is also interesting. Even though I have worked really hard to get where I am in my journalism career, I sometimes wonder if, when people say stuff like this, it means people think it's the only thing I have in my life that is of any worth? I admit that, for a while, I started to worry I'd slipped into this way of thinking too, but thankfully I have stopped seeing my job as my only form of validation.

I wrote about this topic in my newsletter and it is one of the most popular editions I've ever written. In it, I pondered the idea that maybe it's that people feel a bit threatened by or uncomfortable with the idea of a single woman on their own and so need to find a way to explain it to themselves.

I said:

> I do think a part of it is that people feel the need to label others to help them understand, because there is a fear around people not conforming to the status quo. It's easier—and more socially acceptable—to put me in the career-obsessed box as a way of explaining it away. I feel like people are thinking: "Yes, she is still single, but don't worry it's only because she is one of those career women."

Discarding the Fairy Tale and Telling New Stories

In recent years, driven by writers such as Catherine Gray, the author of *The Unexpected Joy of Being Single*, Rebecca Traister, the *New York Times* bestselling author of *All the Single Ladies*, Kate Bolick, who wrote *Spinster*, Shani Silver, author of *A Single Revolution* and Bella DePaulo, who wrote *Single at Heart*, among others, there has been an explosion of work celebrating being unmarried and unattached.

Single positivity even became a watercooler topic in 2019, when actor Emma Watson mentioned in a *Vogue* interview that she considered herself to be self-partnered rather than single. While not revolutionary, her comments were certainly relatable. The Harry Potter star was telling the interviewer about turning thirty and how she'd "had all these ideas" about what her life was supposed to look like at this age. She didn't understand what the big deal was about turning thirty until she was thirty, she said, and felt quite stressed and anxious about where she was in her life.

"And I realize it's because there is suddenly this bloody influx of subliminal messaging around," she said. "If you have not built a home, if you do not have a husband, if you do not have a baby, and you are turning thirty, and you're not in some incredibly secure, stable place in your career, or you're still figuring things out . . . There's just this incredible amount of anxiety." She added that she had never believed people could be happy being single and thought it was just a "spiel" until she felt it herself. "I call it being self-partnered."

*

I spoke to Radhika Sanghani about how writers—and other creatives—have a responsibility to help change the narrative. Radhika is the author of seven fiction books, including *30 Things I Love About Myself.* She told me how she very purposefully made sure that the main characters of her novels "don't end up with the guy."

She says: "It's not that I'm against that, it's just I think there needs to be a wider range of stories. I remember, at one point, I wasn't dating or I had just had a breakup and I wanted to read a rom-com type book, but not one with a happy romantic ending. I found it bizarre how difficult it was to find anything. It shouldn't have to be that hard.

"I just really wanted to write books that were a reminder that you don't need romantic love to feel like you have your happy ending," she says. "I know we all know that rationally, but I feel like we don't actually really know it, because of society's heavy messaging. I can't go off and change the entire plots of all rom-coms and Disney, but what I can do is try and help change things going forward so we have a wider range of stories being told."

That's not to say she won't ever write a book with a successful love story. She tells me: "If something's going well in someone's love life, that's great, but it doesn't have to be the be-all and end-all. I always want to remind people that in literature as much as in life: we are the ones that take center stage in our lives, not our romantic love stories. That's really important to me."

Stories That Defy the Narrative

Here are some recommendations, in no particular order, for what to read or watch if you're looking for something where single people are portrayed positively. Many of these were recommended by *The Single Supplement* community. This is obviously not an exhaustive list, but hopefully a nice jumping-off point.

A Constellation of Vital Phenomena by Anthony Marra
Animals by Emma Jane Unsworth
Careering by Daisy Buchanan
City of Girls by Elizabeth Gilbert
Convenience Store Woman by Sayaka Murata
Daisy Jones and the Six by Taylor Jenkins Reid
Even Cowgirls Get the Blues by Tom Robbins
Ghosts by Dolly Alderton
Girl, Woman, Other by Bernardine Evaristo
Happy Happy Happy by Nicola Masters

In This House of Brede by Rumer Godden
Love Me, Love Me Not by Kirsty Capes
Mistborn by Brandon Sanderson
My Sister, the Serial Killer by Oyinkan Braithwaite
Orlando by Virginia Woolf
Queenie by Candice Carty-Williams
Really Good, Actually by Monica Heisey
Single Bald Female by Laura Price
The Book of Negroes by Lawrence Hill
The Broken Earth by N. K. Jemisin
The Lost Queen by Signe Pike
30 Things I Love About Myself by Radhika Sanghani
What Fresh Hell by Lucy Vine
Wool by Hugh Howey
Anything by Sarah J. Maas
Ali Smith's Seasonal Quartet
Any of Terry Pratchett's books featuring Granny Weatherwax

Alien (1979)
Almost Famous (2000)
How to Be Single (2016)
In Her Shoes (2005)
Muriel's Wedding (1994)
Mystic Pizza (1988)
Prime (2005)
Romy and Michele's High School Reunion (1997)

St. Elmo's Fire (1985)
The Break-Up (2006)
The First Wives Club (1996)

Firefly Lane by Kristin Hannah or on Netflix
Fleabag, British comedy-drama television series
Grey's Anatomy (particularly Christina Yang's story arc)
Miss Fisher's Murder Mysteries
Normal People by Sally Rooney or on BBC iPlayer
Sex and the City (particularly Samantha's storyline, culminating in the first film)

SIX

Getting Left Behind

A few years ago, one of my cousins was getting married in Northumberland. My parents and I decided to travel up to Edinburgh for a visit beforehand. My sister met us in Edinburgh and the four of us then drove down the east coast, stopping at a few places on the way, such as Dunbar, a town on the North Sea coast in East Lothian, where some of my dad's ancestors are from, and Bamburgh, in Northumberland, to see the castle.

As we headed south from Edinburgh, I was sitting in "my" seat in the back right-hand, behind my dad, who was driving the car, and my sister was sitting in "her" seat. We were bickering. And I suddenly had a strong feeling that, because neither my sister nor I have partners, we were kind of trapped in eternal youth. If my sister and I had families of our own, we would likely not be in this car. Our original family would become secondary to our new families. Instead, the four of us still do the same things we did when Rachel and I were kids.

Sometimes this makes me feel like a grown-up kid. As I write this, I'm thirty-eight and I've managed not to hit any of the classic personal markers of adulthood. I haven't got married, had kids, bought a house, or even learned to drive. By the time my mum was the same age, she wasn't just married with a house and a car—she also had two teenagers (she had gotten married and had me and my sister in her early twenties, which was pretty normal for the Baby Boomer generation).

It's not just me, though. Things are changing. On average, millennials are getting married seven years later than their parents, and more are choosing not to marry at all. The age at which women have their first child has also consistently increased over the last four decades, with many millennial women waiting until the age of twenty-nine or older. The homeownership rate among millennials is also 8% lower, compared to the preceding two generations. There are many reasons for this, including the fact that younger generations tend to have higher levels of education (which also means more student debt), and women, in particular, are much less likely to be expected to find a husband in order to have someone to support them. In general, young people are entering the workforce later. Meanwhile, the cost of living has risen dramatically, while house prices have also soared.

Despite societal changes, research from 2022 indicates that the pressure younger people feel to achieve milestones is affecting them more compared to their predecessors. According to Relate, 77% of millennials (ages twenty-five to thirty-nine) and 83% of Gen Z (ages sixteen to twenty-four) feel the pressure to attain these traditional landmark life events.

In other words, people feel an enormous amount of pressure when they aren't doing the things that their families—and wider society—think they should. Newspaper headlines scream about falling birth rates and mock millennials for not being able to afford houses (one memorable headline even put this down to the fact millennials eat too much avocado on toast). As I have discussed at length, there is still a pervading stigma about the unmarried and childless. Things have changed, but not fast enough to alleviate feelings of failure when we don't reach the milestones we are expected to reach. This is made worse by pressure from loved ones and the feeling of getting left behind when our friends reach these milestones ahead of us.

Dealing with Family Expectations

Although we don't speak of it much, I know that my mum would love to see my sister and I find husbands. I'm sure she would absolutely love to help throw us those big white weddings I used to dream of as a kid. I also know my mum would love to be a grandparent. I used to get annoyed with her for voicing that, as I felt like it was unnecessary pressure. Over time, though, I've come to realize that it's only fair that she is feeling that loss. Being a grandparent is a role that many people aspire to when they get to a certain age, and it must be hard when all of her friends have grandchildren to dote on and she has none. Sometimes I feel guilty that I have deprived her of that. I can empathize, because I sometimes feel that loss too when my sister talks about never wanting children. Of course, that is my sister's right, and I support her decision completely, but, at the same time, it means I will never have the niece or nephew I imagined when I was younger. And yet we all have to accept things like this in life. And while I hope that one day I can provide my parents with grandchildren, I can't promise I'll ever come to her with an engagement ring on my finger, asking for help to organize my special Big White Wedding.

I asked *The Single Supplement* Facebook community about their experiences with family. Several in the group told me how they noticed that, while their married siblings get separate wedding invites, they are often still included on their parents' wedding invitations, even when they haven't lived with their parents for years or decades. Others told me about being seated at the kids' table at family gatherings—one even said she was once expected to sit on the floor while her coupled-up relatives sat at the big table—or being given the worst room or even the sofa when on family holidays, while all those in relationships get the nice big double rooms with en suites. In most cases they were also expected to pay the same as the couples.

One of the group members, Gillian Lavansch-Brown, thirty-five, told me: "I'm the oldest of four siblings and get comments at every family gathering about how I'm the only one who doesn't have someone. Some of my family members are always, quite pushily, trying to 'set me up' with someone. They do it embarrassingly publicly, with no subtlety. I also just get a general feeling that they feel sorry for me, even though I'm perfectly content with my solo life."

When I first interviewed writer and podcast host Tahmina Begum a few years ago for an Instagram Live, she told me her parents had accepted she didn't want to get married in her twenties and therefore weren't pressuring her to find a husband, which she noted was unusual, given she's from a Bengali and Muslim family. When I interviewed her again for this book, however, Tahmina, who is now in her late twenties, told me that things have started to shift.

Tahmina, who is also the founder of a beautiful newsletter called *The Aram*, said: "So many people graduate and get married straight afterward in my culture, but I wasn't looking at boys that way when I was at university. Something changed the minute I hit twenty-seven. I think it was because it was like other people around me were getting married and two friends got married.

"My cousin also got married recently and she was thirty-five, and that is unheard of in my community. After that they kind of asked me if there was anyone I liked. I really think they thought I would have a boyfriend by now. I said I still didn't feel ready and my mum was basically like, well, get ready then," she said with a laugh.

Extended members of her family will say to her: "But you're amazing, why are you single?" Tahmina said it makes her really angry, because she thinks people are really asking: "What's actually wrong with you?" and assuming she is the one at fault.

"I think my parents think that too. But they cannot understand the state of dating right now, which is so crappy. They ask why I am rejecting so many men, but the reality is there is nobody to reject. It's not like back in the day, when the men would pursue women and be chivalrous like my dad was. Dating apps are awful. They just can't fathom it.

"The thing is, though, I just don't want a boyfriend right now. I think it's different in Western cultures, but very rarely in black and brown cultures do we just let single women be, so they have seen me get my education and build my career and they are now like: 'Okay, it's time for marriage.'"

Tahmina quotes from Sheila Heti's book *Motherhood*, and says she loves the line that goes: "There is something threatening about a woman who is not occupied with children. There is something at-loose-ends feeling about such a woman. What is she going to do instead? What sort of trouble will she make?"

She has quite a positive approach to handling difficult conversations with elders, though. She argues that building better relations with older generations, who may not understand your life choices, is important. "What I've realized is that you sometimes have to be the bridge, even when nobody's reaching out to you," she says.

Modern Friendships

It isn't only family who can leave us feeling like we're doing everything wrong and that we're getting left behind. It's something I have experienced, quite painfully, with friends. As I've mentioned, I really value my friends. I have nourished and prioritized my friendships. I have also leaned heavily on friends during low moments, which is natural when you don't have a partner to wipe away your tears. It seems I'm not alone. In Claire Cohen's book *BFF?: The Truth About Female Friendship*, she quotes Dr. Anna Machin, an evolutionary anthropologist at Oxford University, who has said that as more women are not following the traditional path of marriage and children, close friendships are fast becoming our "survival-critical relationships." As Machin explains, we need close bonds to survive, quite literally, and close relationships have a profound influence on our happiness, health and longevity. The problem is that in modern society, particularly in the West, we have forgotten how important it is to nurture other relationships in our lives, because we are all programmed to focus on finding our "soulmate" and putting everything into that romantic relationship. Our platonic relationships suffer as a result, and when you are single, you really notice it.

It hasn't always been this way. In *Marriage, a History*, Stephanie Coontz explores how, in the past, love was far from the main reason to get married. In some cultures it was even frowned upon. If love did develop, couples in many societies were expected to keep it on a short leash so it didn't disrupt the wider family and community.

"Until 100 years ago, most societies agreed that it was dangerously antisocial, even pathologically self-absorbed, to elevate marital affection and nuclear-family ties above commitments to neighbors, extended kin, civic duty and religion," Coontz wrote for *The New York Times*.

In the past, friendships, the extended family and the wider community were prioritized. Friendships, Coontz says, were more emotionally central. She points out that studies show how isolated we are becoming and how increasingly people have no one to confide in other than their spouse. There is a loneliness epidemic.

"It has only been in the last century that Americans have put all their emotional eggs in the basket of coupled love," she writes. "Because of this change, many of us have found joys in marriage our great-great-grandparents never did. But we have also neglected our other relationships, placing too many burdens on a fragile institution and making social life poorer in the process."

Knowing this is one thing, but the modern-day reality is that cultivating friendships often slips down priority lists. The biggest friendship tests for me have come during periods of change and, as you get older, those changes become more seismic. Our friends might move away from us, or get married and have less time for us, or they might start a family and feel more comfortable around mum friends than those without kids, or maybe they have had to take on the role of carer to a parent. Even if the reasons are completely understandable and there is no bad blood between you, it can still be hard when the dynamic shifts. All change is a kind of death. Even when the change is positive, you may still grieve the way things were before. When I've experienced it, it has sometimes felt like I have had the rug pulled from under me, which is especially hard to deal with when I don't have a partner at home to also rely on.

These changes can mean you are left feeling abandoned, which is a horrible thing to admit feeling about a friend in adulthood, and yet we would have no qualms saying this if a romantic partner or family member suddenly disappeared from our lives. Of course, not all relationships are meant to last forever, but given the importance of friendship for our health and well-being, it does sometimes seem like we have quite a cavalier approach to things shifting or ending that we don't have when it comes to other relationships, which I think is a lot to do with what we prioritize in society.

When Everything Changes

It can be particularly painful for single people when the reason for the change is down to marriage or children. It can often feel like there is an uncrossable divide between mothers and non-mothers. Woe betide the friend who admits that feeling left behind hurts. The unwritten rule is you are meant to pretend everything is okay and that you are absolutely fine about the fact there is a gaping hole in your life where your bestie used to be.

When Jody Day, the founder of Gateway Women, a support and advocacy network for childless women, spoke to her friends about the heartbreak she was feeling that she'd never be a mother, and later wrote about being the only childless one among her friends who were all mothers by then, she was even more devastated when many of them completely turned their back on her.

"One of the very first big pieces about being childless was in *The Guardian* in 2012 and it was about friendship," she tells me. "I didn't say anything mean about any of my friends and I didn't name anyone and I thought that, naively, I might get more understanding and compassion as a result. Actually what happened was, after the article came out, I was completely ostracized from that part of my social group. I was basically canceled."

She told me: "I have very few friends left from the old days, from when I still thought I was going to be a mum one day. And the ones that have survived are incredibly empathic to me, courageously so, in that they were prepared to hear the really hard stuff."

Since I started on this journey of writing about my life, countless people have privately messaged me or sidled up to me to tell me that they are feeling left out or sidelined by their friends—the ones in relationships or the ones who have had children—but don't feel able to talk about it for fear of losing them completely.

I want to tell them they are wrong. That their friends will understand. But I can't say that for certain now I've experienced what it's like being cut out by friends shortly after I spoke out about the pain of not being a mum soon after they became mothers.

It's not just those who are desperate for children of their own who experienced being left out either. Happily child-free people have told me that their mum friends assume they hate kids and therefore don't include them in anything where their children will be present, leaving them feeling like there's an inner circle of mums in their friendship group. This is despite the fact they would love to be part of the lives of those children.

But it can also go the other way. I know some childfree people who have abandoned their mates when they have had kids because they haven't wanted to hang around with children, and I have heard from coupled-up people who have felt left out by their single mates when they have got married as they no longer get invited to do fun things or go on holiday with them anymore. There is a well of pain surrounding this topic and it often feels a bit taboo to raise it.

When Laura Price, author of *Single Bald Female*, was twenty-nine, many of her close friends were getting engaged or married and buying houses with their partners. She was single and her life was about to change forever. In 2012 she received the terrifying diagnosis of breast cancer. Her book, which is fiction, was inspired by this event and the subsequent treatment she had.

Even before she was first diagnosed, she had been single for most of her twenties. She said: "I did have some relationships during that time, but I was always the single one when all my friends were getting married or getting into serious relationships or having their first baby, so I was already used to that feeling of being left behind, but it was even stronger when I got my cancer diagnosis and I moved back in with my parents for six months."

Laura remembered how, on her thirtieth birthday, which was just before she started treatment, she had dinner with her friends, their partners or husbands and her own parents.

> It was me and four couples and that did make me feel like a child, in a way. I felt left out, that's the best way I can describe the feeling. This feeling then continued for much of my thirties, as more and more friends settled down and had babies while I, for the most part, remained single.
>
> There was also this feeling of loss when it came to my friendships and the way that they were before. You no longer have their undivided attention. Perhaps that is selfish to say, but I had friends that when I met up with them, they were just so distracted by looking after their children, completely understandably, that we just didn't have time to have the same conversations that we had before. I really felt the loss of how we had been.

One memorable time sticks out to Laura. She had been told by her doctors that she could freeze her eggs, but that it would be risky to wait to start treatment. Also, given that her cancer was fed by hormones, the extra hormones she'd need to take to facilitate egg retrieval could potentially also be problematic. She confided in her friends and they suggested a get-together. When Laura—who had been craving time with her girlfriends—arrived, she quickly realized her friends had brought their partners too.

"I had twenty-four hours to decide whether to go ahead with egg freezing or not, and I really wanted to be able to discuss it with them that day, and I didn't get the chance to at all because their partners were at the barbecue too. That's one thing that really sticks in my mind. They weren't being bad friends. It was more that they thought they were just there to cheer me up. But for me, I didn't want to have that very intimate and life-changing conversation with my friends' partners present."

Navigating Feeling Like the Odd One Out

Sara Eckel, author of *It's Not You: 27 (Wrong) Reasons You're Single*, told me about her own experience of feeling like the odd one out. Now in her fifties and married, she still vividly remembers how it felt.

"When I was thirty-five, I felt a huge sense that I was so behind and a sense of thinking I'll never catch up, like there was anything to catch up with," she said. "It's almost like we're all in this race and other people were like, ding ding ding on that path, hitting their milestones and then going on to the next phase and hitting that mark and going on to the next phase. And I was still just pumping and pumping and getting nowhere."

Like Jody, she said some of her friends were better than others when it came to making her feel included and for being really empathetic when she wanted to talk about what was bothering her.

"I had a friend who was really sensitive when it came to this stuff. She'd been married since her twenties and did all the things you are meant to do in the right order and yet was the opposite of a smug married person. I remember that if I was complaining about something, she would always ask questions to find out how I was really feeling. For example, about whether I wanted children. She understood that I was a better expert on my life than she was. And she was just a super supportive friend in general."

Since I began writing about being single, I've noticed that while many coupled-up people have been incredibly supportive, a small handful of coupled-up people have been quite defensive. Occasionally there will be little comments on social media. Perhaps this is because I'm challenging the status quo or perhaps this is because they are feeling insecure in their own life choices and are projecting onto me. I don't know every commentator's motivations, but what I do know is that a lot of single people feel unable to speak up when friends or colleagues have said insensitive things for fear of alienating themselves further or having people assume they are bitter. I wondered how Sara's friends felt about her book, which is a no-holds-barred look at the annoying things people said to her when she was single.

"The book was essentially me battling this sort of Greek chorus of judges who had things to say about me being single and many of the people I was talking about were my friends," she said. "The reaction was mostly supportive, but it did rub some people up the wrong way. I had one friend who said it made her cry, and wanted to apologize to me for the way she had treated me. Another was just like 'No comment,' and I didn't know if that was good or bad. There was definitely some negativity, but luckily it didn't come to blows. Regardless of this, I'm glad I wrote it."

The Other Side of the Story

That isn't to say things go awfully with all friends. Some, despite marriage and babies and other major life events, are still able to make time for their friends, whether they are single or not. And research tells us that those people are likely to be the happiest. Studies show that strong social ties actually improve your lifespan. An Australian longitudinal study of aging found people with the most friends tended to outlive those with the fewest by 22%. In fact, having few to no friends can be as risky for your health and lifespan as smoking fifteen cigarettes per day or not exercising. Meanwhile, close relationships with children and other relatives had very little impact on how long you live. Another multi-generational study on happiness, conducted in the town of Framingham, Massachusetts, found that geographically close friends and good relations with neighbors have the greatest effect.

While there were moments that Laura Price felt that her friends weren't there for her in exactly the way she hoped, she also knows that there were times when she wasn't there for her friends either—times she was busy pursuing her career as a food writer, completing treatment and writing her book. As she didn't live nearby, she wasn't around to babysit or support friends who had postnatal depression or when they had scary trips to the hospital. And, ultimately, Laura credits the support of her friends as crucial to helping her get through her cancer treatment. They were the ones to drop everything and be by her side when she first heard the bad news. And now, ten years on from her first diagnosis, they are the ones who have been there for her now that her cancer is back. In 2022, Laura was diagnosed with secondary cancer, which is incurable, although she could very well live for decades thanks to advances in treatment. Soon after, she married the man she met during the pandemic, becoming stepmum to his three daughters.

Of course friendship is not just about support through hard times, but also about cheering each other on when good things happen too. As well as celebrating her marriage, Laura says friends and family really made the effort to celebrate the release of her book. “They have seen me go through so much and they knew how important it was to me. I spent a lot of years working on it and pitching it and trying to get it published. They knew how important it was to me and how it was also quite personal to me. So they have really done a lot to celebrate that and they’re very proud of me.”

Although I have experienced heartache with some friends, I have also been really lucky with others. My longest-standing best friend, Gemma, has done everything in the “right” way. She married in her twenties, bought a house with her husband, got some dogs and had a baby. And yet, if anything, we are closer since she had her daughter than ever before. I am forever grateful.

And just to prove that sometimes single, childless people are the ones to make their married friends feel left out, around five months after she had her daughter, I was back in my hometown for a visit. I didn’t tell Gemma at the time, but I made it my mission to come back every six to eight weeks in the first year of her daughter's birth, so I could be there for her and also be part of her baby's life. I would just announce I was coming back and see when she was free for a catch-up. That weekend she was coming to my parents' house for a cuppa. On the Friday night, however, I went to the pub with two of our other mates. When I shared a series of funny selfies from the night, Gemma texted me to say she was hurt not to be invited. I felt awful. I'd assumed, because she was a mum now, she wouldn't want to come out. It was a big lesson in not making assumptions like that.

Now I'm back living in my hometown, we're reaping the rewards of hanging on to our friendship when everything changed. I have a really lovely relationship with her daughter, which means so much to me. Living on my own close to town also means sometimes Gem will crash at mine after a night out, proving that single childless friends have their benefits to busy married mums in need of a break.

This reminds me of an essay the writer Anne Helen Petersen published on Substack, called "How to Show Up For Your Friends Without Kids—and How to Show Up For Kids and Their Parents." She wrote it after she realized that every week she talked to or heard from people who felt alienated, lonely, uncared for and abandoned.

She wrote:

> Parents feel like their friends without kids have left them behind and are flaky. Kid-free people feel like their parent friends only want to hang out with other parents, and are also flaky. Parents feel like society is incredibly hostile to them; single people feel like society is incredibly hostile to them; partnered people without kids feel like society is incredibly hostile to them.
>
> All of this is true, because society is just flat-out hostile to all manner of people who aren't exorbitantly wealthy (and even they aren't having a great time). That hostility can force us into a defensive crouch, where it's very difficult to see anything past our own struggles, or to empathize with someone whose struggles feel like things that would make your life easier.

The Hat of Belonging

While I love my friends whose lives look very different to mine and appreciate how we show up for each other regardless, having friends who just get what you are going through and who you don't need to explain anything to is also really valuable. When I first moved to London, one of my oldest best friends, Phoebe, was also single. We had around a year together in the city, being each other's date at events, doing wholesome things like going to craft workshops and walks on Hampstead Heath, and also having many a spontaneous drinking session, where we'd end up doing things like accidentally gate-crashing a stag do or deciding on the spot to go to a gig. Being new to the capital, I was so glad for her friendship. But change is inevitable. By the following September, she told me she was getting together with a guy she'd known for a long time. I was so happy for her, but my heart also sank a little bit because I knew things wouldn't be the same, and I was also a bit scared. We'd been relying on each other quite a lot and I didn't know how I'd cope without her being around so much.

Luckily for me, Phoebe totally understood without me having to say anything, because she had been through the same thing with a friend who, before I moved to London, had been her single bestie until the friend got together with someone and quickly moved in with them. She reminded me that her new boyfriend lived outside of London, so she wouldn't see him all the time. She was right and things didn't change all that much for a while, and by the time they did I was more settled in London and had built up a robust social network. I was also lucky that I got on well with her boyfriend, and they weren't the type of couple to make me feel like a third wheel when we did stuff together, which is always a bonus.

It was after this, during one lonely weekend stuck at home with nothing to do, that I realized I had to put myself out there and make some new friends. It often felt like the weekend is made for families having days out or couples having romantic getaways. While I certainly don't advocate ditching your friends when things begin to change, what I do advocate for is making new friends to add into the mix. Making friends in adulthood can be hard but there is a real joy to it as well. From the absolute gems I met while working at a co-working space to the hilarious friends I made on my journalism course, to the group of male video-journalists who were my best friends for around ten extremely fun and very alcohol-infused months, to the strangers I met while going to climb Snowdon, who I'd later enjoy wholesome weekends away with and trips to see *Hamilton*, I found some amazing people and began to feel a lot more settled in London.

Something that really helped was making friends with other single people who I could be my most authentic self with. When someone is in the same boat as you, you don't have to explain how you feel as much as you do with someone who has never experienced what you have. Studies even show that when we find people with similar experiences to our own, it validates our own experience. This is because, when the things we think or feel are normalized, it can feel life-affirming and actually contributes to greater emotional freedom. The research shows that when we feel recognized and accepted by others, we can actually more easily accept ourselves. This reminds me of something Anne Lamott wrote in her book *Bird by Bird*: "All I ever wanted was to belong, to wear that hat of belonging."

I think that's what it comes down to. When we feel left behind, it makes us feel like we don't belong, which is a horrible feeling. Finding people who are also living their lives outside the status quo gives us back that feeling of belonging and helps us feel less alone.

A few years into my journalism career, I won a place on a journalism program and got to spend three months in Berlin. A mutual friend saw my announcement on Facebook and said she knew another journalist who was temporarily in Berlin, with whom she thought I would get on well. I agreed to be set up on a mate date and arranged to go for brunch with this perfect stranger. I wrote about the experience in the chapter I wrote for *Unattached: Empowering Essays on Singlehood*, edited by Angelica Malin.

I wrote:

> I remember clearly sitting in front of this gorgeous, smart, funny woman who had the same job as me and was also in her thirties and immediately hitting it off. She also happened to be single. Jackpot, I thought! She came into my life at the exact moment I needed her and she taught me about the thrill of making friends, especially single friends, in your thirties.

Aside from being set up on a mate date (which I would love to see people do more of!), I thought I would include some inspiration for how to make new friends if you're on the hunt for your own single tribe. I decided to ask members of *The Single Supplement* Facebook group about new friends they made and specifically how they made them. The results were brilliantly varied. One told me she made new friends through sharing passions on Instagram and getting chatting over DM. Another said she made friends by joining her local choir, while another joined a local ramblers group and began to meet up with members for coffee and drinks after going on a few walks and clicking with some members. Someone else said they joined Facebook groups for specific issues, e.g., a medical condition, and made friends that way (and it makes me so happy that many members of my group have met up in real life and become actual friends!). A few said they made new friends at workshops or retreats or on solo holidays. Several had found mates via Meetup.com. I have recently had success making new friends by volunteering—both by becoming a trustee of a charity and by volunteering for a mental health listening service.

Author Radhika Sanghani has taken making new friends to a new level. Six years ago, she decided to dedicate herself to the task of making new friends after realizing she was in a really different place to a lot of her friends and that many of her friendships existed more out of convenience and habit than shared experiences.

"I felt like we were just staying friends for the sake of our shared history together, and it wasn't about ditching them, but just a case of wanting to have more connections that felt relevant to where I was, and who I had more in common with. But I decided to be quite proactive about it because they weren't just going to land in my lap like they do at university."

Radhika began by being more open and striking up conversations with people she came across, whether that was in a yoga class or with the neighbors in her apartment block or in the queue in a café. "I just started to be really friendly with people I come across. If I spoke to someone and felt really warm and nice, then I would suggest grabbing coffee. I used to think that would be really weird, but if I felt a warm connection, they were feeling that too. Plus it was low stakes. It's not like I've known them my whole life and had been waiting to ask them."

Consequently some of Radhika's best friends are now people she has met since she first began her mission to expand her social circle. She also says that, six years on from first making the effort to make new friends, she still makes a new friend at least once a month. "It's magic and proof that it is never ever too late to make new friends."

The Silver Lining of Being a Grown-up Kid

It's also good to look for the silver linings when it comes to our families too. For a long time, this thought of being a grown-up kid who hasn't left her nuclear family made me feel kind of embarrassed and like I was doing things wrong. But over the last few years, I've realized how lucky I am. The time we get with our parents is finite and, thanks to my long-term singleness, I have got to spend a lot more time with them than I may otherwise have done.

When Covid-19 started sweeping across the world, I realized I did not want to stay in London in my studio flat and so decided to head home to Shropshire. The prospect of a garden to sit in and the fact my parents were about to get their first ever dog, a puppy called Ruby, tempted me, but the main reason was that I was worried about my mental health. Part of me was a little ashamed about this, because so many couldn't escape the capital and I felt like a bit of a wuss to admit I was too anxious to stay on my own, and in all my wildest dreams about moving back to Shrewsbury, which I had been wanting to do for a long time, none of them involved staying with my parents for more than a week or two. In fact, when my sister asked at Christmas, before the pandemic, if that is what I intended to do if I did move back, I replied saying: "Over my dead body." But there I was on March 22, 2020—the day before Boris Johnson famously told us all we must stay at home—being driven back to Shrewsbury by the nicest removal-van man ever. As soon as I saw the sign for Shropshire, I felt my shoulders relax and I knew I'd made the right choice.

What I soon realized was that it wasn't so much them supporting me, as me supporting them. My mum, in particular, was very stressed, as she was working as a community nurse and having to come home to my dad, who has underlying health conditions, not knowing if she was bringing Covid with her. Realizing I could help by lightening the mood, chivvying them to make the most of their hour-long exercise out of the house, and encouraging my mum to curb her obsession with checking the Covid death rates, which was just fueling her anxiety, made me feel the opposite of a grown-up kid.

One memorable moment came when things started easing up. My parents and their neighbors had a socially distanced street party of sorts and were outside drinking and chatting in their driveways while I was inside looking after the puppy. It was nearly dinner time (or tea time, as we say in my family) and I decided to order us a takeaway. It was on its way and they still hadn't come home and so, in a weird role-reversal, I was the one calling for them to come in for their tea and then quite literally going to fetch them when they ignored me. There was me, on the doorstep, yelling at my dad not to hug his neighbor and to get inside the house. It was quite bizarre, but a good moment of humor following months of stress.

I have a couple of other friends who had also decided to decamp to their parents' houses during the first lockdown and, when we have spoken about it, we've all had similar thoughts. When else in life would we have the chance to live back with our parents? Of course something might happen, like a job loss or eviction, to cause us to move back, as nothing in life is ever guaranteed, but for the most part we wouldn't have otherwise got to spend that extended time with them in our thirties. For me, it really was a blessing in disguise.

SEVEN

A Year in the Life of a Single Person

There are moments in the year where I feel more naked in my singleness than others. I can go days without considering my relationship status and then suddenly a certain time of year will approach and I will feel much more alone. January in particular does it for me. In the UK, it's cold and dark and everyone is skint from Christmas, so no one wants to socialize. Consequently I spend more time on my own, as friends in couples cozy up together watching Netflix under blankets (if Instagram is to be believed).

New Year's Eve

There are also special occasions that can have the same effect. For some it's Valentine's Day. For others it's Christmas. Or wedding season. Or their birthday. For me, it's

New Year's Eve. I love how New Year's Eve has the potential to bring people together with a collective reason to celebrate in a way that's unique from a birthday or wedding, where the celebrations are focused on individuals or couples. I also love what it represents. I love the idea of closing one year and opening another surrounded by people I love—truly a way to bookend the years with joy. It feels like an important ritual to me.

I'm sure I inherited this attitude from my great auntie, Joyce, who felt that parties were one of the most important parts of life. And I don't mean that she "liked to party" as a euphemism for drinking. She would only ever have the odd sherry, so it wasn't about loving booze. It was about being surrounded by people, celebrating. She never missed an opportunity to go to a party. She loved to dance and sing and would always wear bold colors—usually bright pink—and would inevitably be wearing some kind of party hat, usually one with sequins, by the end of the evening. The pictures of her at various dos would slip out from between the pages of the countless letters she wrote to me while she was alive (she wrote to me in every country I ever lived, and I called her my greatest ever pen pal). New Year's Eve was one of her favorite nights of the year, and so it was fitting that she ended up dying on that night in 2015. As my cousin shared on social media, in her tribute to Joyce, they managed to squeeze one last party in at her bedside before she passed.

It was easy to satisfy my desire to celebrate New Year's in my twenties, however. Everyone always wanted to do something, whether it was going to a club or a pub outing or even just having a "gathering" with drinks and nibbles in someone's home. I would often have options to choose from. Then, as I got older and people paired off, the invitations began to dwindle. The build-up to the last night of the year began to make me feel stressed. I'd send out hopeful messages, asking what my friends planned to do, and would inevitably receive a "We're just planning to have a cozy night in together" in response. I'd sigh, wondering why they couldn't just do that any other night of the year, and turn to the next person. As people began to have children, it became even trickier. As the years went on, I would invariably be the only single person at a party full of couples, if I was invited to anything at all.

My need to celebrate the last day of the year—and the disappointment when it didn't work out as I hoped—left me feeling a lot of shame about how much I craved proper celebrations on this day when others didn't seem to care as much. Even writing this and acknowledging I have a need makes me feel uncomfortable. Being needy is something I've been accused of by ex-boyfriends and even the occasional friend. But it's taken me a long time to realize that men don't often get called needy. The way it's used against women is a product of the patriarchy (see also the word "desperate"), I feel. Women are called needy when we don't behave how society expects us to, which is as quiet, sweet, easygoing, care-giving people-pleasers instead of individuals with their own legitimate desires, wants and needs. When we try to repress our needs, however, they become bigger than themselves—causing lots of uncomfortable feelings, including anxiety, shame and resentment—when in reality everyone has needs and it's natural to want and need things like connection and community on special days of the year.

Spending the last night of the year alone was something I had tried to avoid at all costs for years. One time, I ended up celebrating New Year's Eve in a pub where I knew only the person who had invited me to tag along with her group of friends. I was so anxious about it that I drank loads before I went and then realized I was feeling a bit nauseous and ended up pretending I was going to make a phone call while I hotfooted it to a nearby McDonalds and stuffed my face to soak up the alcohol before running back. There have been some good ones among the awkward nights, though. When one of my best friends suggested climbing The Wrekin, a famous hill near my hometown, one year, I didn't know what to expect, but I found the walk in the dark, and the magic of joining so many people at the summit, emotional in a lovely way.

Despite this, I still feared spending the night itself completely alone. For several months before it happened in 2020, I knew this fear was finally likely to come true.

There was a creeping sense of dread, an anxious examination of my options and, finally, a resigned acceptance. It was in the middle of the pandemic and I was living alone. Another lockdown was looming. Spending New Year's Eve alone was inevitable.

I worked on the last day of 2020 for *The Guardian*, and although I'd compiled a list of ways to spend my evening, I ended up being so tired from live-blogging about coronavirus that I felt quite detached from the night itself until around 11:40 p.m., when I suddenly decided to do something small from my list to mark the occasion. I pressed play on Annie Mac's DJ set, which she was doing on Instagram Live, and danced around my kitchen until something told me to get outside. It was around ten minutes to midnight and freezing, but I wrapped myself up in warm clothes, put my headphones in, and walked around my neighborhood. It felt a little rebellious somehow. Perhaps because, as women, we are often told we shouldn't be wandering around on our own after dark, and yet there I was all alone and doing just that, on New Year's Eve of all nights.

As midnight approached, Annie put on a remix of a house track called "Brighter Days" by Cajmere, featuring Dajae. I'd never heard of it before, but the lyrics were poignant and yet hopeful. The vocalist was belting out that she dreams of brighter days as Annie talked about how we had survived the year and that, one day, we will have brighter days and things to look forward to again. I felt a rush of gratitude and emotion. Just then someone nearby set off some expensive-looking fireworks. I stood in the middle of the empty crossroads at the top of my street to watch, and tears came thick and fast. But I wasn't just crying, I was also laughing at the explosion of lights overhead, the hopeful music in my ears, and how I very nearly missed this moment. It was beautiful—and I wouldn't have changed it for anything.

That night was a big lesson for me. Not only did I learn that the world wouldn't stop if I had to spend New Year's Eve alone, but I also learned it's possible to experience joy on your own. When you are single, it can be easy to slip into negative thought patterns because you invariably spend a lot of time by yourself with only your own thoughts for company. But what I now know is that, if you lean into what you are lacking, you are at risk of missing out on experiencing joy or stumbling across something amazing, as I would have if I'd sat at home dwelling on what I was missing out on.

Valentine's Day

For some, Valentine's Day is the most painful day of the year as a single person. The build-up to the day means you're often bombarded not only with aisles of cards and presents in supermarkets and other shops, but also V-day–

themed content in newspapers, magazines and all over Instagram. It can be hard to escape. For those who are single and don't want to be, it can be a painful reminder of what you are missing out on.

You can, however, choose to embrace the day even if you are single. A friend of mine who I used to work with absolutely adores Valentine's Day. Whether coupled up or not, she chooses to see it as a celebration of love in all its guises. This reminds me of my best friend's daughter. She absolutely loves Valentine's Day too. During the pandemic she drew me a special Valentine's Day picture and insisted that her mum drive over to deliver it to me. I was so touched.

Galentine's Day is another way to reimagine Valentine's Day. The holiday was created by Leslie Knope, the fictional main character of the TV show *Parks and Recreation.* Galentine's Day has since transcended TV and become established in everyday culture. Although not as well known as the traditional V-day itself, it does seem to have inspired a trend to celebrate other kinds of love at this time of year.

One of my newsletter readers, Emma Squire, forty-nine, a nurse specialist from Dorking, Surrey, has embraced Galentine's Day. She takes turns with her group of friends to host an evening of food and drink. Sometimes her group of friends is joined by her twenty-two-year-old daughter and her mates. Last year they put together an indulgent homemade grazing board and each year they choose a psychological thriller to watch—absolutely no rom-coms are allowed.

"We started the tradition before the pandemic when the relationship I was in at the time was imploding spectacularly and I realized I gained more comfort and happiness from the strength of my female friendship on that day instead of from my partner," she says.

But Emma admits Valentine's Day wasn't her bag even when she was in a happy relationship. She says: "I've always felt very cynical about Valentine's Day, with its overpriced flowers and awful generic set menus in restaurants. I've always joked about seeing couples dining out that night looking like they're on a prison visit—staring at each other across a table, looking awkward and with nothing to say to each other, yet forcing themselves to be there for fear of losing face.

"My biggest antithesis about the whole farce has been the shaming of those that are either single or not in a 'perfect relationship,' as if we are a failure in life."

If you aren't able to celebrate with friends, though, it can be really nice to romance yourself a bit. This year I took myself out to my favorite Thai spot in my town's market for lunch a couple of days after Valentine's, as I was busy on the actual day. I chose my favorite thing on the menu and treated myself to a crisp glass of white wine. I didn't even get my book or phone out to hide from myself. I just savored the food and the time alone while also doing one of my favorite activities—people-watching. I just love seeing how people behave and imagining what their lives are like. On the way home I bought myself some flowers: a big beautiful bunch of tulips. Other single people I know have taken themselves on spa days or drawn themselves bubble baths surrounded by candles or cooked themselves elaborate three-course meals.

Summer Holidays

Another time that can be tricky is the summer holidays. While I do advocate for solo travel, when all my coupled-up friends are off to villas or resorts every July and August for a week or two to lounge by the pool or sea, I can sometimes feel a bubble of resentment rise within me. Solo travel, while empowering and even potentially life-changing, takes effort and bravery. Sometimes I just want an all-inclusive holiday with someone I can relax around and be totally myself with. I can't even remember the last time I had that kind of holiday. Spending summers scrolling through everyone else's holiday photos while I'm sitting at home because I didn't dare ask a friend if they'd be up for going away with me is definitely one of my most annoying habits.

My summer holidays these days usually involve camping with one of my best friends (often in Wales), or going on retreats (especially yoga retreats). Recently I told someone about my plan to go on a yoga retreat in Northern Ireland and they couldn't believe I was going on my own. I bit back the urge to say I didn't have much choice, given most of my friends are married and so would be going on holiday with their spouses. In reality these kinds of organized breaks are the perfect holiday to go on alone, as most other people will also be solo and it's all organized for you. The word "retreat" means you have the perfect excuse to take yourself off on your own if the company is getting a bit intense, although, in my experience, I've only met amazing people on these retreats. Some of them have even ditched their spouses for the week, which I salute.

Other Special Times

For a lot of people, the hardest times of the year can be the ones they most enjoyed as children. One of the members of *The Single Supplement* community, Rachel Leff, twenty-seven, spoke to me about how lonely she can sometimes feel during religious festivals. She's an orthodox Jew and consequently has a lot of major and minor holidays throughout the year where her family and the wider community gather and where she ends up feeling like she sticks out as the awkward oldest child who doesn't have a spouse or as the third wheel when she spends these events with friends.

"I used to love this one holiday we have, called Simchas Torah. It is the holiday where we celebrate our Torah by going to Synagogue and dancing with the Torah scroll. In high school I loved observing the mothers and fathers dancing with their children and seeing my friends and their nieces and nephews," she tells me. "Now it is very hard for me to participate in this celebration. Everyone my age has a baby on their hip and some of the kids I used to babysit for do now as well. It can make me feel very lonely."

Rachel gets through the Jewish holidays by practicing what she calls "emotional preparedness" and knowing when she needs a timeout to decompress or practice some self-care.

Christmas

I relate so much to what Rachel says. Although I love Christmas—and absolutely insist on having a six-foot Christmas tree of my very own and going all out with the other decorations and celebrations—I've started to notice how different my days are to other people's. My sister is also single and childless, and so while my friends have developed sweet little traditions of their own with their spouses and children or their nieces and nephews, our

Christmas Day hasn't changed much since we were kids ourselves. I do, however, love the new traditions we have developed; for example, I now do a lot of the cooking with my dad, which I love. But I do sometimes wonder what it would be like if there were children racing around with their new toys, and it makes me feel a little pang of longing.

I think a lot of us feel like we need "permission"—a partner, a family, etc.—to properly celebrate important moments throughout the year, because that's the only model we've ever seen and that's what we are shown in TV adverts and in films, but it is possible to reimagine these special times.

In the US, Friendsgiving, for example, has evolved as a popular way to celebrate Thanksgiving, because so many people can't travel back to their families for the big day. I have friends who take part and tell me that these alternative celebrations can be just as joyous and full of gratitude as the more traditional ones. This reminds me of the Christmas I spent in South Korea with my boyfriend at the time and my friends. Nothing about the day was in any way what I was used to, but by letting go of the fixed ideas about what the day should look like, I was able to throw myself into this different kind of day and really enjoy it.

Giving ourselves permission to celebrate certain holidays

on our own terms could help us change how we perceive those times. We can create our own versions of the celebrations that have been modeled to us. I mentioned my six-foot Christmas tree before; I remember being on an online panel discussion during the pandemic with my tree behind me and some of the people on the Zoom call expressing their surprise that I had such a big tree just for me. Some people in the community I run also said they didn't feel like they should have one or they felt embarrassed to go all out with decorations when it was "just them" or because they had no kids, but why not? Along with my Christmas tree, I have loved collecting decorations for other parts of my house. It makes me happy and why wouldn't I do something that makes me happy just because I'm the only one to enjoy it (apart from the friends and family I have over to visit). We all deserve to do the things that make us happy!

Celebrating on Our Own Terms

I'd love to see more people give themselves permission to throw themselves into special days. Maybe it's finding or creating a specific holiday and making it "yours," like how single women like Emma celebrate Galentine's Day, or even just Valentine's. Mel Johnson, who runs the Stork and I community, loves Valentine's and each year creates a display with love-themed ornaments and decorations in her home. Perhaps, like the model Heidi Klum, you could choose a holiday and go all out for it, as she is known to do for her Halloween celebrations. Maybe it's setting aside a week or a weekend to go somewhere each year with friends. My friends and I recently enjoyed a weekend in a beautiful cabin for a fortieth birthday and have decided to make it an annual weekend. As one of my best friends, Steph, said, when we discussed wanting to go horse riding some time: "Why do we have to wait for a birthday before we do the things we enjoy doing?"

Maybe it's picking a new destination you've always wanted to go to and planning a solo trip there during the summer, so you have something to look forward to. Being single means that we have freedom, especially if we don't already have children, who obviously make this harder, so it's worth thinking about how we take advantage of that while we have it. How do we make the most of being alone? On vacations, for example, we can get reservations at fancy restaurants or bars much more easily on our own. We can treat ourselves, like I did on Valentine's Day this year. We can do this because we are not beholden to another person's schedule. We don't have to factor in their interests or tastes. We can follow our whims and go on adventures, even small ones. When we're having busy periods at work and life gets in the way, it can be easy to let this go and forget the freedom we have.

Something that helped me was doing The Artist's Way course. This is a self-led twelve-week creativity course created by Julia Cameron, where one of the weekly tasks was to take yourself on a solo date. Knowing that each week I had to choose a date to take myself on forced me out of my comfort zone, especially as I decided to really devote myself to the course and fully commit, so to me, these solo dates were non-negotiable. I ended up having to schedule them into my diary in advance because, if I didn't, I'd always end up prioritizing other things and then squeezing something small in at the last minute. I did all sorts of things during those three months and didn't spend loads. Sometimes my "date" would just be putting my favorite film on and making myself popcorn or having a pamper day at home. I would also go to free festivals and exhibitions that I found in *What's On* guides or did things like go for a walk in a completely new place and get myself a bit lost. One day I took myself to a Korean fashion show that I saw a flyer for and another time I went to the theater alone for the first time—and loved it. I actually think doing these dates really helped build my confidence about spending time on my own, and following my own curiosity and desires helped ensure I was more in touch with who I really am and what I want to do. This, in turn, made me feel more confident being single. They were also the perfect way for me to practice self-love and self-care.

After I first drafted this chapter, New Year's Eve approached. I'd thought of not doing anything again—

which would have been the third year in a row—but I kept thinking back to the conversations I'd been having about not letting being single hold you back from enjoying a special occasion. I decided to let go of my self-consciousness about appearing needy, embrace my no-strings-attached status and do what I wanted. It ended up being one of the best New Year's Eves I've ever had.

I didn't spend loads of money or do anything fancy. I just spent it doing my favorite thing—dancing. One of my lovely Instagram followers once asked me in a Q&A what I do that makes me feel most like myself and, without hesitation, the answer was dancing. I've always been the person who's first on any dance floor. While nothing makes me happier, and I do a lot of dancing on my own, just like with NYE plans, opportunities to dance, in public at least, seem to dwindle as you get older, or at least they have in my friendship group.

Another reason this New Year's Eve was so good was that it was so relaxed. It was just me and my pal Tom, a friend I met during the pandemic, who I've become close to in the last couple of years, and it was one of those amazing nights where you don't really expect much. The ones where, hours before you're meant to start getting ready, you consider bailing and staying home on the sofa. Thankfully I forced myself out and I'm so grateful that I did. After a couple of drinks, we headed to the small basement dancefloor of where we were to literally dance the night away—dancing, and also a little flirting with a few hot guys (Tom and I have hilariously similar tastes in men). We had such a great time. At the end of the night, I did end up having a cheeky snog with a fit Scottish bloke (a bearded one wearing a kilt, no less) but, even without that, it was still just perfect.

I can't think of a better way to start the new year than throwing shapes on the dance floor with someone you love without caring what anyone thinks of you. It was pure joy and everything I longed for in those wilderness years where I couldn't find anyone on the same page as me when it comes to celebrating New Year's Eve. I smiled all the way home.

The next morning I even made it to a cold-water swim with Gemma, to welcome in the new year in a more wholesome way, and the following day, when the weather was better, a large group of us, kids and dogs included, headed to Wales for a swim in the sea there and fish and chips on the beach. It was bliss. All in all, I couldn't have asked for a better start to the year.

Thoughts on Solo Travel

One of the most common questions I'm asked about navigating solo life is what to do about going on holiday. Many want to hear whether I'd recommend going on holiday solo. While I do absolutely love reading a book by a pool—and, like I have said, I do crave that kind of trip sometimes—to my mind, there is nothing like the feeling you get when you navigate your way across a country carrying your belongings on your back, not being able to speak the language, and all the while wondering if you're going to die as the bus or taxi you're in speeds round a corner on a cliff-top road. When you make it to your destination, you feel like a superhero.

My favorite solo trip was when I spent a month in Morocco. I'd long been obsessed with the idea of going there. It started in secondary school. My friends and I would daydream about backpacking across Europe, and I would also advocate for taking the boat from Spain to Morocco while on this imaginary future trip. Perhaps it was watching *Casablanca* that did it. I don't remember. As an adult I would see people heading off to Morocco with their partners for romantic holidays and would feel that familiar pang of jealousy.

One year I realized I had to take a month off from my main work contract—a long story, but quite common in the media world if you aren't a permanent member of staff—and hadn't yet made a plan for what to do. At the time I was in the middle of completing The Artist's Way. Doing the course made me reflect on how I needed to bring adventure back into my life, as that helps me stay creative. What better way than fulfilling my dream of visiting Morocco? I found myself googling flights and realized how cheap it was to get there, and that I could still work while over there. I even found a place on the coast where I could stay for free in return for spending a few hours a day working in the bar. This was it. I was finally going to my dream destination.

Of course, before I could go I had to first get through multiple conversations with friends, family and even strangers about how Morocco is the very last place a woman should go on her own. But I wasn't scared. I batted off their concerns. If anything, the naysayers made me more determined than ever. I also did my research and spent the majority of my trip in rural areas, where I met loads of friendly, welcoming people.

Perhaps the fact I was told not to go is one of the reasons that going to Morocco on my own for a whole month is one of my greatest life achievements. Whenever I think about my adventures there, my heart swells. I think another reason it meant so much to me was because I had spent my mid- to late twenties living abroad and traveling, and then was "grounded" in the UK as I retrained as a journalist, and went through that period of being incredibly broke. My trip to Morocco made me feel like myself again, and it reminded me of what I am capable of.

Jamie Klingler, forty-four, a co-founder of Reclaim These Streets, which campaigns against sexual harassment and violence against women and girls, broke up with her long-term boyfriend in the middle of the pandemic. Going on her first holiday shortly after the relationship ended had the potential to make or break how she felt about her new single status, but she chose a pretty epic destination for it. Jamie, who had lived separately from her ex throughout the pandemic, as he was caring for his vulnerable and shielding parents, saw an online advert to go to the Maldives cheaply if you stayed for at least four weeks, which was the resort's way of making money when most people were still not traveling due to coronavirus. Jamie, who had always dreamed of getting married, booked it straight away and decided to take herself on a "solo honeymoon."

At first she wondered whether flying to the other side of the world during a global pandemic and to such a romantic place so soon after the end of her relationship was the most stupid thing she had ever done. But, before long, she settled in, made friends, and began to enjoy herself.

"Before the pandemic I really did need someone next to me all the time. I wanted my ex in the room even when I was reading, just so that I wasn't alone. And, actually, more than anything that changed during the pandemic, it was learning to like spending time on my own that was the biggest thing that changed for me," she says.

Nevertheless, Jamie is honest about the less than idyllic moments of solo trips. Comparing our own particular situation to others is something that can bring a downer on all of these special times in the year. On a trip to Camogli, Italy, later in the year, she came across a town celebration. There was a big fireworks display and bonfires and lots of people out enjoying themselves.

"The promenade was packed with families and couples. I realized that night that I don't need to stay somewhere if it's making me feel lonely, and so I went back to my hotel and read my book and I was fine. Sometimes you do feel that way and that's okay," she says, adding that the rest of her trip was great.

As Jamie points out, we can always just remove ourselves from situations that make us feel sad or lonely. We can also remove ourselves from social media if we find ourselves scrolling through everyone's picture-perfect vacations. When I am stuck in comparing mode, I try to focus on what I do have and journal about it.

One way to enjoy an adventure that can feel a lot safer and less scary than just striking out alone is to book yourself onto a group trip, such as the ones FlashPack run. Like with a yoga retreat, on these organized adventures the itinerary and accommodation are taken care of and there will be plenty of solo people for you to make friends with. The only downside is that they can be really costly.

Another option is trying a house swap—like the one Kate Winslet and Cameron Diaz do in *The Holiday*—which is obviously easier if you live in your own home rather than a house share. Swapping houses means you'll have a lot of home comforts, and you can get recommendations from a local about where is good to go for food or days out. Although it wasn't a house swap, when I stayed at my friend's flat in Italy when she wasn't there, she arranged for her neighbor to take me out for a drink, recommended a local pool where I could spend the day swimming and sunbathing, and suggested walks to local beauty spots. It was such a lovely way to see a part of Italy I otherwise never would have ventured to.

It's worth pointing out that solo travel is easier for some than others, though. I'm able-bodied and white, so am able to take myself off to new countries without either concerns about access or many concerns about being faced with racism.

In Georgina Lawton's book *Black Girls Take World*—which I highly recommend if you're a woman of color who wants to give solo travel a go—she points out how white Western women take for granted their ability to move through the world and how solo travel as a black woman is a radical act, given the history of how Black people's movements were controlled and—still are—policed.

"We travel to craft our personal identities, especially in spaces where being an unaccompanied woman of color is seen as taboo," Georgina writes in her book. "And we understand, better than most, the responsibility and consciousness related to our movement. We travel for ourselves, first and foremost, but attached to our journeys is the potential to rebuke stereotypes, break molds, trace roots, foster inclusivity, and give back. We travel because we can and that in and of itself is reason enough to go."

I love Georgina's words and her book is so empowering, but I understand some people may still be nervous. So something I always recommend is to start small. Why not pick a place a couple of hours away and take yourself there for a mini break over a weekend? Perhaps somewhere by the sea or somewhere nice and rural—or a bustling city, if you already live in the countryside. It will be good practice and help raise your confidence. You could time it around a gig or theater show you want to catch or simply have some much needed downtime away from screens and entertainment.

One of my favorite recent solo adventures was a trip to a local beauty spot to have a wild swim and a picnic by myself. It was a spontaneous trip because the weather was so good and, when you're freelance, you have more flexibility to ditch work and get outside on a good day. I got the train and then walked for forty-five minutes uphill to the reservoir that I'd read about and had wanted to visit for some time. It was a hot day and there was no better feeling than sinking into the waters (it is a popular spot, so I wasn't swimming there alone, which I wouldn't recommend). Afterward I munched on my picnic and then walked back to the nearby town and had a look around the shops before getting the train back home. It was a simple and very cheap adventure, but it still felt empowering and confidence boosting. If I'd waited for the weekend when a friend could have joined me, I would have not only missed out on the good weather but on the chance to feel like a badass.

Solo travel might not be for everyone, but I wish everyone would give it a chance and get that same buzzy, satisfied feeling I get whenever I do it, no matter how small or big the adventure ends up being.

EIGHT
A Room of One's Own

From the conversations I've had while writing this book and being part of a community of single people, I know that housing is one of the issues that comes up time and time again. While it's not all doom and gloom, for many single people the question of where to live—and how to afford it—is a difficult one. It can lead to us comparing ourselves unfavorably with friends who seemingly are able to easily afford nice places with their partners, and it can add to that feeling of being a grown-up kid if we are living with housemates or even with our parents when none of our coupled-up friends are.

The Joys of Living Alone

Throughout my twenties and well into my mid-thirties, my housing situation was all very temporary—and often insecure—and regularly made me feel anxious. I lived in a range of housing setups, from living on a boat to having a studio flat inside my landlord's house (that had no lock on the door, meaning she could waltz in whenever she felt like it), to a variety of successful and not so successful house shares. I am now living in what feels like paradise—a place on my own. I am incredibly lucky to be able to afford the rent, and this only was feasible when I left London and moved back to my hometown of Shrewsbury.

I also don't mind admitting that it wasn't until I lived in the studio flat inside my landlord's house—which was as close as I could get to living alone in London—that I really started to enjoy my singleness. My years being single and in my thirties in house shares got me down. I felt the weight of how far behind I was in comparison to a lot of my friends—especially those back home, as some of them had been living just with their partners since their early twenties. I was also, in general, unhappier, as this was before my ADHD diagnosis, and I was doing a lot of masking to pretend I was "normal," which I had to keep up at home as well as at work. When I had my own space, I didn't have to do this as much and it made a huge difference to my well-being.

I now live in a two-bed terrace house with a cellar and a garden. I have an oak dining room table, which my dad and his friends lovingly restored for me after it had been dumped in an outbuilding where they volunteer. I have my own spare room, which I use as an office. I own a beautiful bed. The mattress is absolutely perfect for me (and I didn't have to compromise with anyone else on its firmness). I have all my stuff in one place. All the decor is my own, I wake when I want, I cook when I want, I have friends over when I want. I have two beautiful cats who follow me everywhere and greet me at the door when I come home. I eat weird things standing up in the kitchen when I want. It's all a dream come true. Well, it would be if I owned it and could paint the walls.

Living on my own is high up on the list of things I love about being single. For those who have never experienced it—and I know how lucky I am to be able to afford it—there is nothing more amazing than being able to relax into being completely and utterly yourself 24/7. Now, I know some people will say, "But I can be that with my husband" or "My flatmate and I have this kind of relationship," but even in the best of situations, you still have to factor in another person and their wants, needs and desires. You have to consider what they want to watch on TV or that they hate when you leave the kitchen in a mess or that they might have an opinion on what you're eating or wearing or doing. Being able to lean in to your true authentic self without having to take anyone else into consideration is a gift. Nothing calms my nervous system more than coming back to my empty house, which to me really feels like my sanctuary. I know I would find it hard to give up.

On rare occasions, I have been on the receiving end of pity for living alone: "you poor thing, having to live there by yourself." If only they knew how much I relish it. I think it especially works for me as I love to get out and socialize, but if I'm around people too much I get overstimulated and overwhelmed. Having my own refuge to come home to helps regulate those feelings. It's my haven. A little place where, when I return, it feels like breathing a big sigh of relief. I also now feel totally safe in my house. That may seem strange, as I know others really struggle with living alone because it makes them feel vulnerable. For me, having been in a very toxic relationship where, when we briefly lived together, I felt on edge all of the time, it's living alone that is my happy place.

I'm not alone in feeling this way. Emily Morris, the author of *My Shitty Twenties*, a memoir about becoming a single mum in her early twenties, wrote a guest piece for my newsletter about living alone, and more specifically it was about how much she loves her bed and having it all to herself.

She wrote:

> I used to long for company in bed. Some people are scared of the dark or of heights; I was scared of being single. How did it feel to be clasped by a warm human being instead of icy loneliness as you drifted off to

sleep? I couldn't remember, and maybe I would never know, and that kept me awake at night.

Not long afterward, I discovered that my anxiety had not only been preventing me from sleeping, but lying to me, as I embarked on a serious monogamous relationship. Although my partner never moved in with me, he stayed over often, and soon our "sides" of the bed were silently but firmly established.

Like most relationships, ours had an expiry date. It had been two-and-a-half years, and I took the inevitable sadness to bed, where I discovered a vast continent of comfort and beautiful seclusion. The cool side was mine, whenever I wanted to fling a limb on to it, my body free to stretch into satisfying shapes. My bed held me and comforted me and, long after I was over the breakup, became one of my favorite places to be. Bedtime was no longer just a part of my routine, but an act of daily pampering.

I've now been single for three years, and in that time I've realized that being single is definitely nothing to be scared of. I've also gradually collected a cache of precious things that make bed even more heavenly: a weighted blanket with a velvety cover, an eye mask, a silk pillowcase, an oil diffuser, various meditation apps, a sunrise alarm clock.

All of those things can be, and are, owned by people who share their beds with another, but I believe they best serve one. I want to wallow in my bed, luxuriate in it, not lie still in a narrow patch allocated to me like a parking spot.

The Downsides of Living Alone

If I imagined what my life was going to look like when I was a kid, I would have assumed that, by my late thirties, I'd be living in a nice home I owned. I'd be able to paint the walls any color I liked and have a nice garden filled with my favorite flowers. Even though I love where I rent, it's not the situation I imagined for myself and it can sometimes be hard not to compare myself to coupled-up friends, most of whom own what I think of as "grown-up houses."

In the UK and other countries, home ownership is still seen as a defining status symbol—and what everyone should be striving for—but house prices are so high, and it can be difficult to save up the necessary deposit when the cost of living continues to skyrocket. Home ownership has been my goal ever since I left London and moved back to Shropshire. Sadly, it still evades me. When I did try, I was outbid by couples able to pool more of their savings to put in a higher offer than I could manage. Buying on one income really is difficult, especially when freelance, and sometimes I find myself getting down when I see people who I know are on lower incomes than me buying houses with their partners. I often think that some of these people take for granted how lucky they are. Even when I've been looking, I've faced estate agents talking about "you guys," as they assume I'm buying with someone. When they realize I'm buying for myself, they've also expressed surprise that I want to get a two-bed just for me. Ideally I'd actually like a three-bed.

Of course it's not impossible to get on the housing ladder alone, but those who do manage it may not end up in houses as nice as their coupled-up friends because it's just so much harder to buy on one income alone, and many of the people I know who have done it have had to make sacrifices on size or location that those in relationships haven't had to make. I know I'll probably get priced out of my area when I do try to buy again, which is sad, because I love it here and I've worked hard to build connections within the community.

While living alone is something I enjoy, it can be stressful knowing it's all on my shoulders, especially when it comes to having to pay all the bills myself. This includes the whole cost of the internet and 75% of the cost of the council tax (single people only get a 25% discount). A house also costs just as much to heat whether one person is living there or two. According to Office for National Statistics (ONS) analysis, people aged between twenty-five and sixty-four who are living on their own spend an average of 92% of their disposable income, compared with two-adult households, who spend only 83% of theirs. They also found that people living alone are more likely to be renting, and feel less financially secure than couples without children, with fewer reporting they have money left over at the end of the week or month.

Single people, on average, are paying £7,564.50 a year more than their coupled-up counterparts on basic household outgoings, according to analysis carried out in 2021. Ocean Finance compared the typical monthly costs for single and coupled-up Brits, including utility bills, rent and the monthly food shop, using data from the ONS. The analysis showed that household monthly bills are £363 more expensive for singles, with rent the biggest contributor. On average, a single person is paying £674 a month on rent in the UK, whereas couples are paying £866, or £433 per person. It's really expensive to be single, especially if you live alone.

It can also be hard because I'm always the one who has to make sure there are teabags and loo roll in the house. I always have to remember my key. Even if I have had a really long hard day, I still have to do all the cooking and tidying myself. There is no one else to pick up the slack if I'm ill. People often talk about the "mental load" that women have to carry, even if their husbands/partners do share the housework. There are countless articles and memes about it and they all assume that everyone reading has a partner who isn't sharing the burden of making sure there is food in the house and that the bills are paid. These articles don't take into account the millions of people of both genders who live alone and so therefore automatically have to carry all of the mental load, as well as the physical load of actually doing the chores. The only thing we don't carry is the resentment against partners not pulling their weight and, for that, I am forever grateful.

The other thing that I don't think gets discussed is the burden of not only doing all of the house admin and shopping, but also the weight of making every single decision for yourself. Not having anyone to discuss pros and cons with, or to bounce all the different options around with. These can be small things, like not knowing what to cook for dinner and wishing I could just say, "Do you have any ideas?" or bigger things, such as buying expensive furniture, or deciding where to live and whether to buy that house.

Fears About Living Alone

One thing I often get asked for is top tips for living alone, which I have included at the end of the chapter, but I want to address some of the main concerns here. A lot of people tell me that they want to try living alone but are scared they will get lonely, or they worry about what would happen if an intruder broke in, or they fear that they will die and get eaten by Alsatians à la Bridget Jones. Others fret about more mundane things, such as if they get the flu and need some medicine, who will help them out? Or what they would do if something happened, like their pipes burst and they didn't know how to fix it?

These are all valid concerns. Just the other day I experienced one of these very situations. It was late at night and I did something stupid. I am a teeth grinder. When I'm really stressed, I do it more than usual, which can leave my jaw and neck in pain all day. It was one of those days and I decided some tiger balm might help my aching and tight muscles, only I couldn't find my little pot of the magic stuff. All I had was some deep heat spray that I had bought and never used. Figuring it couldn't hurt, I sprayed it on my jaw and neck. I realized immediately that something was wrong. A red-hot, itchy rash soon spread over the area and then it got worse. My whole face felt hot and began swelling up, and my chest and shoulders started to feel prickly. I was burning up. I stripped off my clothes, headed to the bathroom, and had a cold shower in an attempt to wash off the spray. That helped a bit, but the red burny rash was still spreading. I started to panic.

I sent a WhatsApp message to my friend Ellen, asking if she was still awake. I thought she would still be and I also knew she wouldn't mind receiving pics of me half-naked. It wasn't that I didn't know what to do—take some antihistamine as soon as possible—it was just, in that moment, I wanted someone else to know what was happening.

When you live with a friend or have a live-in partner, it feels more natural to say, "Oh my God, look at this crazy rash," and part of me did hesitate when I sent her photos of me and my rash. "Am I just attention seeking? Do I really need to bother her?"

Ultimately, though, I know that, firstly, she understands me and knows sometimes I just need to share. Secondly, although she isn't single now, she has had periods of being single and living alone so she totally gets it. And, thirdly, she won't judge me anyway for needing a bit of sympathy because we all need and deserve that.

Although Bridget Jones utters that famous Alsatian line when talking about whether to give up and accept a permanent state of spinsterhood or not, I do understand the genuine fear beneath it. In 2016 I lived in Berlin for three months, as I'd won a place on a scholarship scheme where British journalists could go to Germany and experience what it's like to live there and work in a German newsroom. Although I love Berlin and I had some brilliant times while there, the experience was marred by a bad bout of depression. This was triggered by the fact I was lonely, I hated the job and had had my confidence really knocked there, and I was also worrying about the state of the world. It was the year of Brexit and, while I was in Berlin, Donald Trump got elected. I woke up the day it was officially announced and felt like all hope had been sucked out of the world. I didn't want to leave my bed and I began to spend an awful lot of time in the Airbnb I'd rented for the period of my scholarship.

Two of my best mates from home came to visit me, which broke up the monotony and loneliness and cheered me up. But during the visit one of my friends got stuck in the bathroom. The studio flat had been designed by architects specifically for weekend visits, but thanks to changes in the law, the owners were forced to rent it out for longer periods, which was how I came to be living there. It was a really cool design, but aside from the interconnected wooden furniture, it was like living in a concrete block. After we'd struggled to get my friend out of the bathroom and finally released her, I got back into bed and my mind went to a dark place. I realized that, if the door jammed while I was there alone, I would be trapped. The bathroom walls were heavy concrete and the door to it, which was a ceiling-to-floor door, was incredibly thick. There were no windows. If I had no phone on me, I would surely starve to death. Thanks to my incredibly vivid imagination, I was able to picture the scene perfectly. I imagined the initial creeping sense of dread and how much I would panic, and then surely I'd end up just being resigned to my fate. I couldn't imagine anyone finding me in time. The newspaper where I was essentially doing work experience didn't seem to notice or care that I hadn't been turning up thanks to being depressed—and I didn't see the few friends I knew in the city enough for them to worry or check on me in time. I was also only calling my parents once a week. From that moment onward, I began to take my phone everywhere with me and also left the bathroom door ajar.

It was such a palpable fear that it's had a big impact on me. It didn't help that I'd also stumbled across a news story of a woman, on holiday alone following her divorce, who got trapped in an airing cupboard and died. I now check in regularly with my family on WhatsApp, I'm in touch with friends all the time, and I take my phone everywhere. I still leave the door open when I go to the loo if I don't have any visitors. I also know all my escape routes should there be a fire and I try to make sure my house as a whole is as secure as possible should anyone try to break in. Now that I've been living alone for a while, however, my fears have abated and, like I said before, I genuinely feel safe. Occasionally, when I'm walking down the stairs, which in my house are very steep, I'll worry about falling down them and being unable to call for help. But for the most part I have control over these kinds of worries and can be more rational about them. I also have an Amazon Echo, so I could call for help through that.

As for concerns about being lonely, I think that depends on what kind of person you are. I love living alone, but living alone is good and works for me when I can invite friends and family over or go out to spend time with people. I make sure I schedule face-to-face time with loved ones, as well as chatting to friends over the phone or voice notes on the days I'm not seeing anyone. As much as people slag social media off for being too addictive, I think there is also a lot to be said about how connected the apps can make you feel. I can't imagine living alone if I didn't have WhatsApp.

The longer I've been single and the longer I've lived alone, the longer I have accepted that it is okay to feel lonely sometimes. It doesn't mean I made a terrible mistake living alone. It's a normal part of life. Sometimes points during the year will make it feel worse. I've mentioned in a previous chapter that I find the winter months, particularly January, especially hard. Everyone is feeling the pinch after Christmas and no one wants to leave the warmth of their houses. The weather, and the fact it gets dark so early, feels oppressive. I feel trapped in my house all on my own. But now that I know this about myself, I can make sure I seek out opportunities for connection and social interaction.

This year I focused on exercise and my social life became twice-weekly workout sessions with friends. I also continued to swim—also with friends—and planned some nice things to do on weekends, including cooking for a group of friends at my house, which was a nice, low-cost but really lovely evening. Making some new friends who also live alone, like my friend Tom, who I spent New Year's Eve with, has also made a difference, as they were more likely to be available and want to socialize, so I had a couple of cozy nights in the pub as well.

Even with the added concerns that come with living alone and the additional financial pressure, I still wouldn't have it any other way. Like most things, practice makes perfect. You get used to it and, if you have the right support around you, it doesn't really feel that lonely. It can instead feel absolutely liberating and even joyful to live alone. There is also a sense of satisfaction you get from working it all out and realizing you can do it for yourself, which is something those who have never lived alone won't experience. It makes you feel so confident and capable, and you also realize how resilient you are. It's a powerful thing to know that you can look after both yourself and your home.

Living with Others

But what if you simply can't afford to live alone? There are quite a few options. You could live in a house share with strangers, live in a house share with existing friends, live with parents, live in a shared commune or warehouse or boat community, or be a lodger in someone else's home. You could even be a guardian of a building that's empty, which is a popular thing for young people in London to do. I have done most of these myself.

What was important each time was making sure I felt that my personal space felt like my own, so I had somewhere to go that felt like a refuge. When I was a lodger in a very small room, that involved pinning colorful postcards and posters to my noticeboard. When I lived on a boat, it was about making my bed as cozy as possible with my favorite bed linen and blanket. House plants and splashing out on fancy candles also made things feel more like a grown-up space rather than still feeling like I was a student at uni. Wherever you live, we all deserve to have a safe, warm home that feels like our own, even if we don't actually own it, and even if there are loads of other people sharing the space.

Living in house shares or with parents is increasingly common among people well into their thirties or even older, thanks to the cost of living and the housing crisis, which is pricing many people out of living on their own. The number of people aged thirty-five to forty-four sharing flats actually rose by 186% in just five years between 2009 and 2014, according to the flat-sharing service SpareRoom. More recently, SpareRoom stated that there had been a 239% increase in fifty-five- to sixty-four-year-olds looking for house shares between 2011 and 2022, and a 114% increase for the forty-five to fifty-four age group.

The Downsides of Living with Others

I spoke to some members of the single community about how they feel about their living situations. While some people had positive experiences, many wished they could live on their own.

For some it's the instability of flatmates moving in and out that is difficult to handle. Lucie, who is thirty-eight and works as an analyst in an accountancy firm, has lived in London for the last ten years in a flat with a revolving cast of three others. Prior to this, she lived in the Midlands and was able to rent a flat on her own.

"If people move in and out frequently, the dynamic changes and you're always having to factor in the behaviors and timetables of other people," she says.

"There used to be a sense of community in the flat but, post-pandemic and with a change in flatmates, it feels increasingly like people leading individual lives under the same roof."

For others, it's more the lack of privacy that gets them down. Rachel, twenty-six, works in data and modeling for a UK high-street bank and lives in London with three other single women. The experience, she says, is a nightmare, but she can't afford a place on her own even though she would like to.

Living in house shares has had a negative impact on her mental health. "I'm more of an introvert by nature and I hate that there's no real privacy," she says. "I also particularly hate that I have to live the majority of my life in a single room. It is sometimes nice to have company, but at this point in my life I would love to have more space and be able to relax after work outside of my bedroom without having to socialize with housemates I don't want."

Added to this, there is a lot of tension in the house. She says: "Two of the women in our flat don't get on and there have been constant arguments and passive-aggressiveness, which I was often called to referee, and now one of them has ended up falling out with all of us, which makes it incredibly awkward."

*

While the traditional marker of adulthood in the West used to be for people to move out and start their own homes from around eighteen onward, recent analysis of UK Labour Force and Resolution Foundation data by the *Financial Times* shows that, in Britain, only around one in five eighteen- to thirty-four-year-olds have a setup like this. The most common living arrangement for young adults now is to still be living at home with their parents. But it's not just younger people who live at home. There are growing numbers returning to the family fold after living elsewhere, due to their circumstances changing.

Louisa, thirty-one, lives in Bristol, is digital learning designer at a university and lives with her parents, who are in their sixties, and her brother, who is in his thirties and has autism and is unlikely to ever be able to live independently.

I asked her how she felt about her living situation and she said she had "sort of" accepted it, but finds it very frustrating. "I can't see a way that it's affordable for me to live alone, and would rather live with family than live in a house share with other people," she says.

"However, it is very frustrating to want to be able to live independently and not be able to, as a women in her thirties on an average salary, and it also makes me feel infantilized somewhat, living in my small childhood bedroom, although I know I am lucky to have this option."

There is another layer to her frustration. "I've known from a young age that, eventually, I will probably be responsible for my brother's care, so it is also frustrating not to be able to have years of independence beforehand and be financially secure. This is a constant worry."

She admits to being "pre-emptively defensive" about negative comments, but says she is "quite open, as I want people to realize that it's becoming a more common occurrence, and it's not a choice because I'm lazy or expect my parents to look after me."

The Joys of Living with Others

Living with others can absolutely be a positive experience, though. Writer Becky Barnes, thirty-six, who is the author of *The Uplift* newsletter on Substack, went from being a homeowner to moving back in with her mum in Kent after living alone for five years. Like many others, she had a big reevaluation of her life post-pandemic and decided to quit her job, sell her flat and leave London. She has since moved to Brighton, where she is retraining as a psychotherapist and lives in a house share.

"Becausc I had quit my full-time job, I could not afford to get another property on my own, even though I had been a previous homeowner, which I'm sure many single people also struggle with," she says.

Even though it was a necessity, she says the seven months back living with her mum was positive, and she was able to be there to help care for her mum while she went through chemo. Becky was also determined not to slip into acting like a teenager and that, instead, they would be two adults sharing a home. To achieve this, they had some open and quite challenging conversations about boundaries, and regularly checked in to see how it was going.

Most of Becky's friends now have children and live in family homes with their partners. She says that, while comparison is inevitable when friends' lives look different, she has managed to get to a good place, where instead of comparing herself with others, she is focusing on herself, after the time back at her mum's gave her the space to do a lot of self-work.

"I've been through my own journey after seeing most of my friends have children when I don't," Becky says. "But during this time, when I had the safety of living with my mum, and my mum just made the space for me to do a lot of soul-searching within myself, I have come to a place where, more often than not, I truly am not comparing myself to other people anymore. Instead, I'm just focusing on designing a life that feels good for me."

*

Mae, twenty-seven, is a business journalist and has been long-term single. She lives with four other people in Manchester and loves it. They share a "massive" Victorian terrace, meaning there is enough space for everyone and the rent is cheap. One of the other benefits she gets is the life advice from her older housemates.

"They're all in their thirties and forties, which has been great, because they've all lived life longer than I have and offer me advice on work-related issues or relationships when I need it," Mae says. "My friends are hitting the big milestones, like buying houses, getting married and having children. Having that additional support network outside of my family has made a difference and given me perspective when I most need it."

*

Others choose to live with others in order to foster community and connection. Sarah Weiler, thirty-eight, is a DJ, a leadership coach in schools and the host of the *Knowing When to Quit* podcast. She lives in Brighton in a beautiful four-bedroom house with three other women, aged between twenty-four and fifty-two, which she calls the "Creative Residence-sea."

"I was living alone in Hackney," she says, "and was unexpectedly asked to leave the flat last August. This prompted me to ask myself what I needed, aged thirty-eight, as a single woman. I didn't want to fit into an existing flat share—that felt like a step back. I also was feeling quite lonely living alone.

"During a visualization in a coaching session, the idea came to me that maybe I could find an entire property and choose the people myself. I drew what I wanted and found the exact property a few weeks later in Brighton. I then put together a PDF of the sort of home I wanted and trusted the right people would find it. They did! A total leap of faith, but it's paid off."

It's more than just a house share, Sarah says. "It's a space to support people's creative projects as well as have a feeling of family for people without a traditional setup. The house is big enough to host events. We regularly bring people together for singing days and are also hoping to run meditation circles and even day retreats."

Shutting Down Comparison

One of the things that a lot of people I spoke to brought up was how crap you can feel when you compare yourself to friends and peers, even if you are relatively content where you are. It's something I still experience even though I live alone. When I visit a friend's house that has a huge beautiful kitchen with large bifold doors opening out into the garden and a cozy reading nook, I feel that pang of jealousy and think of my own small kitchen, which feels so inadequate in comparison. In reality, my kitchen is absolutely fine. It's only when I compare it to others, that I notice its faults.

It's also worth remembering that sharing a home with a partner can be really challenging, especially if you have different ideas about decor or who does the cleaning or how much messiness you're willing to tolerate. I know women who do literally everything around the home. Someone else pointed out that children actually make the worst housemates. Those with kids have no time to themselves, have to constantly tidy up and clean up mess, and most of the time this labor is invisible, so these little—or not so little, if they are teenagers—housemates aren't even grateful for the efforts that go into making their house nice and comfortable.

Something that also helped when I was living in less than ideal situations was to remind myself that nothing is permanent. It might feel like things will never change, but they will. Maybe one day I'll have a kitchen with a reading nook and floor-to-ceiling glass-paned doors out into my garden, but, in the meantime, I'm going to count my blessings for the home I do have and do everything I can to make the best of it.

Tips for Feeling at Home in Any Space

Here's my advice if you're living alone for the first time:

When you first move out, it's definitely worth scheduling in coffee dates, dinner or drinks with friends or family to ensure you have reasons to leave your house and have some social interaction in the diary.

When you have unpacked and made the flat your own, you could invite your friends over for dinner. When I first moved into my house, I set the date ahead of time and it helped me stay motivated while unpacking and getting the house looking nice.

Having things in your calendar to look forward to will help on the evenings where you might feel a little at a loss with what to do with yourself. On those evenings, I try to do something nice for myself, like rent a film or run a bubble bath with lots of candles or cook a new recipe and buy something fancy for dessert.

Put on an audiobook, the radio or a podcast. It can feel like you've got company. You could also call a friend for a chat, but forcing yourself to have a few nights without any interaction will help you get used to it. After a while, it will become normal. I still love to listen to podcasts when cooking, though. I find it really relaxing.

Introduce yourself to your neighbors and slowly build up a positive relationship with them. It can make all the difference to know there are people nearby who know you. Try to be helpful. Join your local Facebook group or start one, if your neighborhood doesn't have one already.

Eating alone doesn't mean you have to just do something quick and convenient. You deserve the care and attention of cooking nice meals that you would give to someone else you were cooking for. Challenge yourself to try a new recipe a week. Have nights where you cook yourself a three-course meal, just for you. It feels decadent and almost wrong, because we're so used to not treating ourselves or thinking we don't matter enough, but we do matter.

Make sure you have house or contents insurance, in case something goes wrong. Think about your escape routes if there was a fire, and make sure your windows and doors are secure. Something I've been meaning to get is a doorbell with a camera attached, which fellow live-aloners have said makes them feel safer when answering the door. Make sure someone else has your spare key, in case you get locked out. Try not to obsess about all this, though.

Here's my advice if you share your living space:

Make your personal space your own. Buy some lovely things for your bedroom, such as nice candles, house plants and throws. Think about the lighting and invest in some lamps and fairy lights. Make it your own sanctuary.

Have a chat with your housemates about how you'll use shared spaces and the decor. This is important, as it can lead to resentment. A friend once moved into a house where a couple already lived. They were all on the tenancy agreement, but the couple treated it as if it was their home and all the decor in the shared spaces were their own, leading my friend to feel like a guest. It was not ideal! Obviously, if you are living with your parents or are a lodger in someone's house, this is trickier, but having an honest chat about whether there is anything they'd be willing to compromise on to make you feel more at home could help.

If you don't eat together each night, schedule in a time when you do have a house meal together. Take turns to cook. It's hard living with a total stranger, especially if you have different work schedules, so making time to talk and break bread together can help. If it's your parents, this can be a nice way to show off your culinary skills—if you have them—and remind them you aren't still a teenager but a grown adult.

On that note, why not organize to do things outside of the house as a group once in a while? Perhaps you could all go to the cinema together or just to the pub. Even if you don't see these people as your friends, some bonding time can go a long way.

Regularly check in and raise any issues before they lead to resentment. There is nothing worse than a passive-aggressive housemate who has been pissed off about something for ages but has not communicated about the problem in a healthy way.

Don't shirk on cleaning and tidying. And come up with a plan to make sure you all keep on top of the housework.

Try not to compare yourself to your friends or let family members get you down about where you are living. One thing that helped me in the past was to practice gratitude and remind myself of the ways in which I was lucky to live in a nice warm and safe environment. I also reminded myself that comparing myself to someone else's highlight reel was always going to make me feel blue. Very few people will be 100% happy in their living situation and there are downsides to all circumstances.

If your goal is to live alone one day, or even buy, think of a way you can remind yourself that it will happen at some point. I had an arty postcard pinned to my noticeboard in my last house share of a lovely room in a house, which to me represented "a room of one's own." When I got down about my living situation, I would look at the postcard and remember that it wasn't forever, and would visualize myself in a lovely house. I still have that postcard and it reminds me of the power of having a vision and staying hopeful.

NINE

Being an Independent Woman

There's a famous saying that "behind every great man there is a great woman." I would argue that it goes both ways. Even if people don't want to admit it, I think that behind many great women is more often than not a really supportive and financially solvent partner cheering them on, enabling them to take career risks, try new things, and generally offering a safety net and buffer.

I remember, when I first became a journalist, I got to know a couple of writers who had book deals. Both admitted to me that they couldn't have done it without the financial backing of their husbands, who paid for everything while they took time off to write. Great, I remember thinking, I'll never be able to write a book if that's what I need. I couldn't imagine ever being with someone who could financially support me while I took a few years off to work on a project that may or may not end up being fruitful financially. Nevertheless, even a partner unable to do that would still be someone who could help share the bills and offer emotional support.

Coping with Everyday Challenges

Everyone experiences shit weeks. Everyone has run-ins with difficult colleagues or tensions with friends. Our boilers might break or we might find out our cars haven't passed their MOTs. Our mums may have really annoyed us or we have had a shock looking at our bank balance. Someone might have been rude to us at the supermarket or a neighbor might have kept us awake partying all night. We just might be really knackered and feeling emotional. These day-to-day challenges we all face are things that those in couples usually talk through at night with their partners, perhaps over dinner or in bed. A problem shared is a problem halved, as the saying goes. So who do single people tell? We can tell our friends or family but often I've struggled with this, as either the issue feels too trivial to make your busy friend listen to you moan or it's an ongoing problem and you risk boring the hell out of your mates.

A while ago, when I was still in my twenties, I was struggling with my job. I had a nightmare boss. The goalposts were changing all the time. I was undermined. I was yelled at over the phone and hung up on if I raised a problem. More often than not, he was actually the reason for the problem, but somehow he always managed to act the victim and sidestep any blame. He also had an uncanny knack of having selective amnesia about any negative feedback he received, and so therefore never altered his behavior. A classic narcissist, he was always right about everything. It was so stressful and, at the time, thoughts of how to handle the situation consumed me. When I spoke to friends, all I wanted to do was bitch about my boss. But I could sense I was doing it too much. I was like a broken record. But I had no one at home who was obligated to listen to me. I struggled with having no one to offload onto.

In the end, I quit the job. But sometimes I still think about how much single people internalize and carry. Of course, if we could afford it, we could all get therapists. But it isn't the same as someone in your house every night asking how your day was.

BBC presenter Salma El-Wardany, who is also the author of *These Impossible Things*, spoke to me about the challenges of being single. While she fundamentally believes that being single is easier than being in a relationship—because you only have yourself to worry about—she knew to expect moments of pain during her years of being by herself.

"Like anything, there are ebbs and flows to it," she says. "There's some periods of singledom that are just exquisite and then there are also hard periods and periods that are difficult. It's just the same as in a relationship."

Sometimes a painful moment would creep up and surprise her. She remembers a time when she had worked a fourteen-hour day and had to go grocery shopping on the way home, and knew she'd then have to cook her dinner herself when she finally got in. Money was tight at the time, and this was something that made Salma, who is from a working-class background, anxious, as she had no safety net.

"As I was walking home, and I was knackered from the day, carrying this heavy bag of groceries, I knew that I would get home and there would be no one there to take the bag out of my hands or to give me a cuddle and say, 'I know it's been a shit day but I'm going to look after you tonight.' That was a hard moment and it happened a lot. I'd get home and be faced with absolute emptiness. I compare it to standing in a vast marble hall and you say something and it just echoes back at you endlessly, because there's nothing and nobody there."

Salma says that learning to "self-soothe" was how she handled the hard times. It helped when she let herself cry and sit with her feelings, rather than denying them. "One of the most valuable lessons I learned during my years of being single was learning to self-soothe. In those moments I would really look after myself. I'd do lots of self-care and nice little things for myself. And then I'd call my girlfriend, crying. Suddenly, when I'd say it out loud to someone, I'd feel so much better and it would feel manageable again."

It was Salma's ability to survive tough moments like this that led a former lover of hers to describe Salma as "the closest living thing to a goddess" he'd ever met. This wasn't in praise of her beauty or grace—although she has both—but because she lived alone, paid her own way and wasn't afraid to demand what she wanted. She adds: "Yes, it can be really fucking hard, but hard things are what teach you and so it's also phenomenal to be single."

Getting through everyday challenges alone is something radio presenter Maia Beth thinks those in relationships take for granted. Maia—a rising star at BBC Radio 1, where she presents a pop show—knows all about this. Despite being in her early twenties, Maia's journey into her dream career has not been easy. I first met Maia when we were paired together by Second Source, an organization set up to support women and non-binary people in journalism as a response to the #MeToo movement. Maia, who at the time was a journalism apprentice for a major broadcaster, was matched with me. I provided mentoring and a friendly ear as she tried to make it in an industry that is notorious for being dominated by privately educated Oxbridge graduates. We bonded over feeling like imposters in our respective jobs.

As I was working on this book, I wanted to speak to Maia about how she succeeded in such a tough industry without a partner at home propping her up—or any family nearby. "I have friends who are also breaking into this industry, but they are living with partners or with their partner's families or their own families. All of my family are in the northeast and I'm single, so I don't have that in-built support, which would also take the pressure off."

The thing that bugs Maia is when people don't appreciate how lucky they are. She told me: "I come across all sorts of people in my work, and one woman was telling me about how her husband had given her the gift of having two years off without work. I was screaming internally. I thought, 'Good for you, but don't call that a gift. It's a huge privilege.'"

She says: "I have definitely missed having that emotional support, but I've sort of adopted this mindset that I do everything for myself, and so I'm very independent and I always think, 'Well, I've got this far on my own.'"

When the Going Gets Tough

One of the things that people often worry about when they either think about becoming single or are newly single is how they will cope on their own if something terrible happens.

When I think back to the worst moments of my life, many of them happened while I was single, so for me it isn't like I have memories of how much better it was to have a partner by my side when things were going badly. I've just had to handle it, and, as I've already discussed, I have been supported by amazing friends and family.

I think it's easy to romanticize that everything would be better with a partner, though. I've done this on many occasions. Sometimes it's happened when there hasn't been one truly terrible event but just during a bad week. Sometimes I have thought about it when my depression has reared its ugly head, which it does every few years. But thinking back to the times when I've struggled, if I'd had a partner to consider too, I honestly think it would have made me more stressed, because I would have had to factor someone else in. There is, of course, the possibility that they would actually help. It certainly would be good if there was someone to make me a cup of tea when my depression kicks in. In my experience, though, having suffered with bouts of depression when I was in relationships, being with someone didn't really help. If anything it just made it worse. This is perhaps because, as a recovering people-pleaser, I used to try to push down how I was really feeling to make sure any boyfriend I was with was happy, resulting in not managing my symptoms well and feeling resentful and neglected.

Now, a few years into my diagnosis—and the additional

diagnosis of ADHD—and after two years of psychotherapy, I feel much better equipped to handle my low periods. And thanks to being freelance and working from home, I have to do much less pretending. After decades of pleasing people to ensure none of them abandoned me, I've got healthier boundaries with friends and I'm much happier in general, which I think has come from truly getting to know myself and listening to what I need. I also have many more nights at home, rather than being out drinking all the time. I now really value spending time at home on my own or with one friend, sitting on the sofa nattering with a cuppa in hand. I also love other wholesome ways of spending time with friends, such as going swimming or for long walks or to exercise classes with them. I feel like I've really developed my own tool kit for when things go wrong.

But What If Something Truly Catastrophic Happens?

Lorna Harris, who is writing a book about grief and works in charity-sector PR, had been single for around three years when tragedy struck in 2018. She lost both her parents within six months of each other, leaving her totally without an anchor.

"My brothers had their families to go back to. I knew they were going to go and cry in the arms of their wives, and I just didn't know what to do with myself," she says. "I actually texted my mum, even though she was dead, and said, 'I don't know what to do.' I felt really low, but in the early stages I just kept thinking of what my mum would tell me if she was still there. Nothing could have prepared me for losing them both within six months, but you become a person you didn't know you could be. You end up incredibly resilient, and since then I've become quite good at coping with my grief."

Lorna moved to the seaside town of Whitstable in Kent in 2019, after living in east London, close to her parents, for most of her life. It was something she'd long dreamed of. She knows her parents would be proud, because she'd talked about always wanting to do it when they were still alive.

"Life has gone on. It has to," she tells me. "I've achieved so much and moved to the coast, and I have this amazing sense of freedom now. If my dad was still alive, I'd be still in my flat in London. My life was fine there, but I didn't have a reason to stay after they'd both gone."

When she was packing up ready to go, a friend told her that, by moving to the coast, she would have to graft to be part of the community. It's not like moving to a big city. You have to work to be accepted in a smaller town. "I took that seriously and called it my adult freshers week. I joined a choir and made loads of friends that way. I went to a grief group. I made best friends with my neighbors, who moved in on the same day as me. I've really thrown myself into it and it's helped me with my grief. I'm never not grateful or proud of myself for making the leap after losing mum and dad, especially as a single woman."

*

Kris Hallenga, author of *Glittering a Turd*, who sadly died while I was editing this book, knew a thing or two about finding silver linings. Her social media feed often featured cats, wild swimming, fun outfits usually involving glitter, travel pictures and videos of silly dancing. But that's not all. Kris was the founder of the awesome charity CoppaFeel, which she started after getting diagnosed with terminal breast cancer when she was in her early twenties. For Kris, it was getting ill—and terminal cancer is one hell of a big turd to be dealt with—that actually made her realize that she could be happy alone.

First diagnosed in 2009 when she was twenty-three, she was single for most of the time she had cancer, and she also lived alone. Well, alone apart from her cat, Lady Marmalade. Early in her experience, she did meet someone and had a relationship, which was featured on a BBC documentary about her life, called *Dying to Live,* but the relationship wasn't meant to be.

"I realized I had to concentrate on myself," Kris told me, in an interview for this book. "Any ill health forces you to focus on what's important, and what was important was getting better. After a while I realized I don't need someone and I still feel joy, but it wasn't until I was in that extreme situation that I realized I could still be happy on my own. I actually didn't think it was possible before, and I wanted to cultivate that idea a bit more.

"I've become an expert in understanding what makes me happy and what doesn't make me happy, and I've realized it is in my own power. I don't know if I would have realized that without getting ill and being forced to look inward."

From the outside, Kris was clearly surrounded by love and seemed to have an army of good friends and family supporting her as she continued to go through treatment and hearing terrifying scan results. She agreed: "I think connection and being with people that really matter, that is love. When you can sift out the shit and you're left with the real gems, and you love yourself enough to know you're worthy of that love and you deserve to spend time with them because you've chosen them: that's real love."

Like Lorna, Kris found that living by the coast also helped in tough moments. She often took herself down to the sea when things were going badly. Spending time alone also helped her process bad health news. "I love living by myself and I relish time alone," Kris told me. "I know when I need to get away from other humans and spend time in my own head, and I'm not afraid to do that, but I also know when I need distraction, and I know who to call when I need to surround myself with people. I cope because I can be on my own and I cope because I have the option not to be. Having a twin also does help, as we really are doing this life together."

The Fear of Dying Alone

A few years ago, a book about dating was published. The title was—and I wish I was joking: *How to Not Die Alone*. I'm sure I wasn't the only one to flinch at the title. It felt like scaremongering. "You better sort things out and find a man—by parting with your cash for my advice—or you will not be able to escape this fate," it seemed to say. But there was another reason some who were single found it so uncomfortable—the title actually expressed one of their deepest, darkest fears.

The thought of growing old and dying alone can be so hard to talk about and can make people feel really emotional, but it's also hugely important. I asked members of *The Single Supplement* community to anonymously tell me how they really felt about it. Responses ranged from people saying they were "terrified" and "worry about it every single day" to "I try not to think about it."

One, aged thirty-eight, said: "[I'm] honestly terrified. It keeps me up at night. I'm an only child with no extended family and chronically single." Another said: "Being disabled and an only child, it feels like my only options are to force myself to find a relationship or end up in a nursing home when I'm older." Another said: "I'm terrified of being a burden to strangers or siblings but unsure why I think that fear wouldn't exist if I had a partner."

Other members of the community had slightly different fears. Those with children were kept up at night by the thought of dying or becoming seriously ill and leaving their children alone. Those who were single mothers by choice felt this most keenly. One told me: "We are all petrified that we will die and our children will be left in the house alone, scared and hungry, etc. We have all been discussing how to try and ensure we have backup should anything happen. We have been teaching our very young children what to do if Mummy doesn't wake up . . . We have told our childminders, nurseries and neighbors to come knocking if we don't appear one day."

Some of those who responded pointed out that having a spouse or a large family was no guarantee of being helped if they were to get sick. Their partner might be useless when it comes to care or they might get estranged from their children. One person said they knew of people whose children didn't agree with the care they themselves wanted, which was making them feel like their wishes won't be respected if they were to become incapacitated. Another said they knew someone with four children who still ended up in a care home with no visitors.

Social isolation among the elderly is rife, and this is often in spite of the person's relationship status. "I don't see this as a single-person issue but a society one," one respondee said.

This is something that was echoed by a number of others. One said: "It's not about not having a partner at that point, it's the lack of a community around me, and as I age not being able to do the things I enjoy now. Having a very active life now and lots of wonderful friends and connections, I fear those dwindling and being left alone in a space with none of them. The fear of that future is profound."

Not everyone was that worried. Quite a few people pointed out something I always remind myself of, which is that being in a relationship is no guarantee of not dying alone. I wrote about this for my newsletter when I did an issue about "How to Not Die Alone":

> Most couples don't actually die at exactly the same time. Life is not like that scene in *The Notebook*. Unless you both die in a terrible accident, the chances are that one of you will die first—and if you are a straight couple, it's the man who is more likely to be the first to go (given the statistics on life expectancy), so even if you have been married all your life, by the time you die you will probably be widowed and therefore single. At least those of us who have been long-term

single will have had lots of practice by the time we reach old age.

*

Another interpretation of that scaremongering book title is that the author thinks we should be worried about actually dying on our own without someone who loves us by our side. Firstly, there are also a million ways to die that would mean either being alone or being surrounded by a bunch of strangers (e.g., car accident, on the operating table, etc.). This just isn't in everyone's control. Secondly, if we could choose who was next to us when we died, if we were terminally ill, for example, why does she discount all the other people that can love you, such as your parents, your siblings, your best friends?

Still, worrying about growing old was a common concern. Some members of the community have tried to mitigate those worries by making contingency plans. One said she had researched retirement communities, while another was making sure she made decent contributions to her pension. Another reader said that, despite being in good health, she was already preparing power-of-attorney paperwork. Another said she had openly discussed her fears around growing old with her family, so they were aware of her wishes. Others have said nieces or nephews have already promised to look after them. Some had even thought about the merits of assisted dying, while others are choosing to be proactive and are focusing on their health and fitness, so they'll be in the best possible shape as they approach old age. My favorite responses were from those who had already made plans to buy houses with best friends in older age, in order to grow old together. I love that idea.

Asking for Help

Something that members of *The Single Supplement* community tell me is about how hard it can be to be single when you either fall ill or get injured. Suddenly you find yourself in a position of needing to ask for help, which can be really hard for a bunch of people who are so independent.

When single people are in trouble or ill, they can feel more vulnerable. Tola Doll Fisher and I met when we were invited to be guests on a podcast about personal finance just before Christmas in 2019. We clicked immediately. She's such a warm, positive person, so I was astonished to hear her story, which she wrote movingly about in her book *Still Standing*. Tola's newborn baby tragically died, and just six months later her husband left her. She went from being a married mother to being neither in an impossibly cruel space of time. And yet had picked herself up and was, through her TED talk and book, inspiring others who experienced hardship not to give up either. Just a few years ago, however, fate dealt her another bad hand when she was diagnosed with cancer.

Getting such a terrible diagnosis is always going to be hard, but being single can make it harder. "When you're sick, and you're being told something important about your diagnosis or illness, it's a lot to take in and often you don't think of the questions that you should ask because there's too much to think about. If you have a partner who's a bit removed from it, because they're not physically going through that, they can then be that spokesperson for you, so when you're single you don't have that and you have to ask for help," she said. "It can be really uncomfortable to ask for help, but I took my cousin's husband with me last year and he was so good at asking all the little details."

Something else Tola wishes she had thought about before getting ill was having income insurance, which would have stopped her getting into loads of debt. "I would have been protected and, as a single person, when something like this happens and you can't work, you just don't have any income. I think this shows how people can really suffer in society because they don't have the protection of a partner."

I asked readers of my newsletter how they felt about asking for help. One said that she thought the fear of asking for help was actually a fear of rejection, while another reader, Claire, suggested a shift in perspective about what it means to ask for help can make it easier. She said: "I heard once that by not allowing someone to help you you're actually depriving them of the opportunity to do something nice, which will make them feel good! As much as I hate asking for help, I often think of the idea of reframing the situation."

This made me think about all the times I could have reached out for help but stopped myself. Was it that I really thought no one would help? Or was I making assumptions? Perhaps my independent streak was just making me stubborn, or perhaps I was actually scared of rejection?

Now, anytime I find myself thinking that no one would want to help me, I remind myself how I would react if a friend or neighbor reached out to ask me for help. And I know that I wouldn't hesitate to say yes, and that it would make me feel good to be able to help them. I think most of us want to do anything possible to help another person in need. Why not give someone that chance?

When Having a Partner Hinders You

Sometimes having a partner at home can actually hinder you rather than help. In many heterosexual relationships, women are still expected to shelve their career plans when babies come alone, whether they want to or not. They are also still the ones to shoulder the burden of looking after the house and cooking the meals. A YouGov study conducted in 2021 revealed persistent disparities in the division of household responsibilities and childcare within couples. The survey found that 38% of women who work full time and have a partner reported bearing the primary burden of housework and childcare, while only 9% of their male counterparts reported the same responsibility.

There is also a growing body of research that shows that women end up doing more of the mental and emotional work compared to male partners. They're the ones keeping track of when everyone needs to go to the dentist, worrying about childcare during school holidays and keeping on top of everyone's schedules. Lots of women I know tell me that their partners or husbands simply don't worry about these things. Others feel like they live with an adult baby who needs everything done for them. Doing it on your own is one thing, but doing it for your live-in partner who won't lift a finger is another kind of draining.

The relationship might also be a bad one, abusive even. Their spouse might not want them to have a career or might be threatened by their success. They might just be so focused on keeping their erratic partner happy that they have no energy left to try to achieve the things they want to do. Their partner might enjoy putting them down. I have experience in the latter: one of my exes enjoyed telling me it was unlikely I'd ever write for *The Guardian* and that I should be more realistic about my ambitions. (Reader, that was in 2013. I was first published by *The Guardian* the following year and I've been writing for them almost continuously ever since.)

This was something I talked about with the British actor Rebecca Humphries. As discussed in an earlier chapter, Rebecca was famously plunged into the spotlight when her then boyfriend, a famous comedian, was photographed cheating on her while he was taking part in the BBC's *Strictly Come Dancing*. After feeling like she was being silenced by the narrative around the scandal, Rebecca released a statement on Twitter (now X), in which she described how her boyfriend had treated her prior to the incident. A statement which, it is safe to say, has gone down in history as an example of a woman really taking back her power. Rebecca has since gone on to write a bestselling memoir, *Why Did You Stay?*, which explores toxic love, emotional abuse and finding self-worth.

In her author bio for the book, Rebecca lists her achievements, which include writing for *Vogue*, speaking at the House of Commons, starring in *The Crown*, *Friday Night Dinner* and the UK's remake of *Call My Agent*. The final line of her bio reads: "All of the above has happened following her public break up in 2018."

What a line. A total chef's kiss moment. Reading her book, it's clear that her career wasn't going well while she was in that relationship. She was out of work and was struggling with auditions, so it's very pleasing to see how much she has risen like a phoenix out of the ashes. It also goes to show what can be achieved when you escape unhealthy situations and can focus all your energies on yourself.

She agrees, explaining how she felt when her relationship imploded publicly. "When it happened, I didn't have anywhere to live," she says. "I didn't have any money. I was financially reliant on him. And, of course, I didn't have a boyfriend, which was the thing that I was taught in my life that, if I had, it meant I was winning. And there I was without that anymore. It was a scary world. Suddenly you realize that you've got to start again."

The experience led her to make other realizations too: "I suddenly thought that I've really got to do the work on what it is that makes me happy and how I define that. And then I can start choosing and curating my life and how I use my time in a completely different way.

"Thinking about the success I've had in my career, it has arrived to me once I started realizing that success has nothing to do with being validated by anyone else. It's about happiness. Success has everything to do with checking in with yourself and seeing what is making you happy and what ignites you. When you haven't got all that weird residue, you can really focus on what you want and, lo and behold, it tends to lead to success."

The Importance of Celebrating Yourself

Over the years that Maia Beth and I have known each other, I have been continually bowled over, watching her star rise as she moved from news toward her dream of becoming radio presenter, culminating in her taking on Mollie King's maternity cover on BBC Radio 1, which was announced the day after we spoke for this book. Although I didn't know what the news was, it's safe to say she was buzzing. I asked Maia how she celebrates exciting moments when on her own.

She told me:

> I think that's one of the best things that I've learned from being single for the last four or five years now is that you can celebrate yourself. If I get good news or I've had a good day, there are lots of people who want to celebrate with me, and we can have a big party, but on a personal level, above all, I will also find a way, even a tiny way, to celebrate myself. It could be as simple as going to buy a nice bath bomb and have a really special bath with candles.
>
> You've just got to make everything a "main character" moment. That's what's really nice about being single.

> You're not having to wait for someone else to do it for you. You can just think: if I'm in charge of this, I'm going to either do something for myself or I'm going to get a bottle of Prosecco on the way home and I'm going to call my friends and tell them to come over and we're going to dance in the kitchen. You have the power, you have the control, and you don't have to compromise.

I absolutely love the idea of having "main character" energy, as Maia puts it. In fact, when she said it, I had a bit of an epiphany about how I often don't act this way when I should. This realization then reminded me of the scene in *The Holiday*, where Kate Winslet's character, Iris, realizes that if her life was a film, she would be playing a side character, after the older man she has befriended, Arthur, tells her: "You, I can tell, are a leading lady, but for some reason you are behaving like the best friend."

Iris replies: "You're so right. You're supposed to be the leading lady of your own life, for God's sake! Arthur, I've been going to a therapist for three years, and she's never explained anything to me that well. That was brilliant. Brutal, but brilliant."

I'm also reminded of an agony aunt column that Dolly Alderton included in her book, *Dear Dolly*, which collected her columns for *The Sunday Times* of the same name. In it, she is giving advice to someone who writes in and asks how to better support their single friends.

As well as tips on how to support your friend if she is ill or having a hard time, she adds: "Bad times are bad for everyone but good times are hard when you've got no one to celebrate with, so make sure someone's celebrating with her. Check if she has someone to have dinner with on her birthday, especially if her family live far away."

Like Maia, Kris Hallenga was also an advocate of celebrating yourself. It's fair to say that Kris prioritized celebrating her life and all her achievements, whether that was her birthday, her book launch, her "Cancerversary" or simply the weekend. Usually these celebrations involved her and her twin sister, Maren, wearing a lot of glitter and sequins. Or they involved wetsuits and dips in the freezing ocean. Before she died, Kris even hosted a Living Funeral—or FUNeral, as she called it—which featured Dawn French in her *Vicar of Dibley* role, an ABBA singalong and a silent disco—as well as moving speeches and a eulogy about Kris's life. It looked absolutely amazing. And made me think about how sad it is that we wait for someone to die to talk about how much they mean to us and how much we loved them.

I told Kris that some members of the single community have told me that they feel sheepish or even embarrassed that they want to celebrate work achievements or birthdays or things like buying their first home. I've even seen people wondering if they are being selfish for wanting to throw a big party when it's just them, or others who feel like they should wait to do things like this until they have a partner to do it with.

Kris couldn't believe her ears when I mentioned this. "It baffles me. I'm perplexed that anyone would think they didn't have the right to celebrate or that it's only valid if they have someone," she said. "Celebrating comes naturally to me. The motivation isn't so much 'Fuck it, I'm on my own. I don't care and I'll do whatever makes me happy.' It's more a case of 'I don't need to wait until some magical time to celebrate things.' If you're waiting to celebrate some kind of joy until you're with someone who can make it more valid or meaningful, you might be waiting a long time, and you might never get to celebrate anything. For me, it's all about relishing moments while you can."

*

In many respects the themes discussed in this chapter are the ones I most wish my coupled-up friends and family members could understand. Doing everything alone, coping both with day-to-day challenges and when the shit hits the fan, adds another layer of stress that those with supportive partners might not fully understand.

Worrying about having to ask for help when there is already stigma about the way we live our lives can also play on our mind. Then there are the concerns about the future and growing old that those in secure long-term relationships might not worry about as much.

On the flip side, celebrating our wins as independent women can also be uncomfortable—and, from the conversations I've had and my own experience—can actually make many of us feel even more lonely than during harder times. Of course, the only real solution is to be honest about how we are feeling. The more we do that, the more the single experience will be understood by others.

TEN

The Mother of All Questions

The first time someone called me maternal, I was in my early twenties and living for a short time in the US in Washington state, on Whidbey Island, to be exact. I was staying with my cousin Suzanne. She and her husband and son had already been living over there for decades and I went to have an adventure, as, at this point in my life, I hadn't yet built up the courage to do a proper solo trip.

During my stay, Suzanne's sister, husband and their young children also came to stay. We were headed to Seattle for the day, to do some sightseeing. As we were on an island thirty miles north of the city, this involved a ferry ride and a drive, plus lots of walking from the most convenient car park. As we all piled into two cars to go, I noticed the youngest child of the group didn't have a jacket with her. It was a beautiful sunny day in late May, but I thought she might be cold on the long journey home, especially given we had to go on the ferry.

“Hang on,” I said to Suzanne, as she switched on the engine, “I’ll just grab her a jacket, just in case,” and then I leaped out of the car. When I got back, Suzanne turned to me and said: “You’re just like your mum: she was always so maternal even before she had kids of her own. You’re going to be such a great mum.” She beamed at me. I blushed, but as she turned back to start the car, I couldn’t help but smile too as I looked out the window. It was a sweet little comment that she probably instantly forgot making. I didn’t say anything, but my heart sang at her words, although at the time I didn’t feel in any way ready to make it a reality anytime soon.

A few weeks later, toward the end of my time on Whidbey, I traveled to the mainland to visit the Skagit Valley tulip festival in northwest Washington with Suzanne and her friend Melinda, who I had grown close to during my stay. On the way we stopped at a cute little shop that sold soft toy rabbits as well as rabbit storybooks and clothing adorned with rabbits. For some reason, we all got quite giddy and giggly and picked up lots of the toy rabbits, which were incredibly soft and squishy. While Suzanne, Melinda and Melinda’s daughter decided they wanted to buy one, I hesitated.

I’d been holding one of these cute little rabbits, but then put it back, feeling embarrassed. “Get it,” Melinda said. “You want it, so why not?” I did want it, but it felt silly to want it. I was neither a child nor anywhere near having a child of my own. What did I want with this squishy bunny? And yet Melinda was right. After a bit more dithering, I bought the toy with a vague idea of gifting it to someone's child when I got back.

That was fifteen years ago, and I'm still yet to give the bunny to any of my friends' kids. I have considered it—it's perfect for babies or toddlers. It would have made the ideal gift when any one of my best friends had their first babies, especially as I haven't seen soft toys like them over here. I almost did give it to the baby daughter of one friend, who actually owned rabbits. But I stopped myself every time I thought I might do it. If I'm honest, it's because I know what I really want to do. I want to keep it for my own child that I still don't have. And so it's still with me, and sits at the back of a shelf, out of sight in my bedroom.

I'm currently thirty-eight and so I'm now way past that scary age of thirty-five that everyone goes on about, when your fertility is meant to fall off a cliff. While that famous statistic has been disputed, the odds are nevertheless stacked against me, and yet I have always felt so certain that I would one day be a mum and that it would all work out. Despite this, I sometimes catch sight of that fluffy toy when I'm tidying or looking for a book and I wonder if I'm wrong. What if I never have a baby to give the bunny to?

The writer Nell Frizzell describes how the years between twenty-five and forty are defined by the constant hum beneath every decision you make, big or small, and that hum is doyouwanttohaveababy? In her book, *The Panic Years*, she wrote: "The panic years can hit at any time . . . During this time, every decision a woman makes—from postcode to partner, friends to family, work to weekends—will be impacted by the urgency of the one decision with a deadline, the one decision that is impossible to take back: whether or not to have a baby."

The concern that it might not happen for me has become almost deafening in recent years and turned into a full-blown ache. Sometimes the fact I want to be a mum but I'm not yet a mum is physically painful to me. It feels like a weight on my chest. Sometimes it makes my stomach churn with fear. If I let it bubble up, I actually feel panicky. There hasn't been a day that's gone by since I turned thirty-one that I haven't thought about it. There's a famous meme of a woman looking confused while trying to work out some maths equations—that's what it's been like in my brain as I've wondered whether I should try to find a boyfriend to have a baby with, even though I don't currently want a relationship, or if I should try to find the money to go it alone with a sperm donor, and then wondering how on earth I would afford it after the baby arrived. This underlying worry has shaped my life for the last few years, and it has been exhausting. I know, at times, I have also been a bad friend because of it, as I've let it consume me, leading me to be, at times, irritable and selfish.

Feeling Ambiguous Toward Motherhood

Many women go through the Panic Years unsure of how they feel about motherhood. One of the members of my community, Ellen Kang, an occupational therapist who works in mental health, who is based in Perth, Western Australia, told me about her mixed feelings. In her twenties, she didn't think about having children, and it was only in her thirties that she gave it more thought.

She said:

> A part of me liked the idea of the traditional household and another part really didn't want to be a single parent, as I am very used to being independent and having the freedom to do what I wanted. I also think that I saw that my mum gave so much of her life and her identity as a mother and I didn't want this for myself.
>
> That's not to say I didn't appreciate what she did as a mum. It was not easy for her, being a first generation immigrant from South Korea who didn't speak much English when she moved to Australia, but I had some ideas about feminism and wanted gender equality from a really young age.

Despite this, turning forty has made her reflect even more. In fact, it took her by surprise how much that milestone birthday made her do this. Having grown up in arguably one of the most isolated cities in the world—Perth—she has no regrets in prioritizing her travel goals, and for the opportunities she has had in her career, but sometimes she does wonder about the route she hasn't taken.

> I've lived in different places, including spending my mid-twenties in London, and these experiences, and being single for most of it, have absolutely shaped me in a different way than I can imagine I would have been if I'd been in a long-term relationship and had children. I definitely have moments of grief for what-might-have-been, even though this could be a million different possibilities.
>
> If I had to choose, I'd say that I'd prefer a wonderful long-term relationship over a child, but who really knows. I just want societies around the world to see all people for their inherent value and not place so much importance on whether someone is single or not, or a parent or not.

Choosing to Be Childfree

Some people know instinctively they don't want children. Even though the choice is often a positive one, choosing to be childfree still carries with it a lot of stigma.

Members of *The Single Supplement* community told me that people often tell them they will change their mind or that they will end up regretting it. Some have been asked if they aren't worried about having no one to look after them when they are old. There's also this pervading idea that if they don't have children they must be completely selfish, and also that they must live a footloose and fancy-free life with no worries at all.

Another reader of the newsletter, Marianne, who works in research administration at a university and lives in Baltimore, has known since she was a young girl that she didn't want children. "Ironically, I once told my mother and some of her friends that if marriage was solely about procreation, which was their position, then I would never be married because I planned to never have kids. They laughed and told me I'd grow out of it. Here I am, still single and child-free at fifty-four."

I ask her if she remembers what influenced her views. "There are a few things that probably impacted my outlook," she tells me. "I grew up in a very chaotic household, as the youngest of five children, with some siblings who had violent tempers. I was super introverted and spent a lot of time trying to stay out of the way. I think that experience, as well as seeing the toll raising kids took on my parents, just made the whole idea of parenthood seem quite negative. I have also never been comfortable around or interested in babies."

I asked what the best thing about being childfree is and Marianne tells me: "Honestly, looking around the world today, I cannot imagine the fear and worry that must live within every parent. And the oh-so-heavy responsibility of having to try to raise a kid to be a thoughtful and responsible member of society under circumstances and pressures so vastly different from when I was a kid. More practically, though, I expect it is just the freedom. Freedom to not always have to put someone else's needs ahead of my own. Makes me sound a bit selfish, but that's the truth."

Shani Silver, author of *A Single Revolution*, told me in an interview for my newsletter about her experience of being vocally childfree. By being so open about it, most people in her life have stopped commenting on her decision or asking her to explain herself. "Also, I like to think we're getting better collectively at accepting 'I don't want to' as a valid answer," she told me.

My Panic Years

My Panic Years, or The Fear as I call it, really began for me when I was thirty-one, following that pretty disastrous visit to a relationship coach. I'd first begun to panic on my thirty-first birthday, when I woke up in a box room of a flat where I was lodger, and the scary age of thirty-five, when a woman's fertility is meant to drop off a cliff, suddenly felt alarmingly close. I thought to myself: "How am I ever going to have a baby?" I pushed The Fear down and went on with my day, but after leaving the coach's office a few months later and realizing that she was right, and that I should hold off trying to date because trying to find a boyfriend really wasn't going to fix any of my problems, I also suddenly knew something else for sure: I wasn't going to be a mum anytime soon. I remember standing on the street outside the offices following the meeting and this thought making me catch my breath.

Realizing I didn't want a boyfriend anytime soon, but that I did want a baby at some point soon-ish, are two not ideal things to suddenly know at the exact same time. For a few weeks—or it could have been days—I walked around in a bit of a haze, until one night while working a night shift at *The Guardian* that was really quiet, I decided to google the problem. I came across a blog by Liv Thorne about her decision to become a solo mother by choice, using a sperm donor. I read as much as I could before I had to go back to writing articles and I sighed a breath of relief. I thought: "Oh, okay. Here's my back-up plan. I'll do it alone!"

After sharing this with a couple of friends—my first real confession that I wanted to be a mum and that it was worrying me that it might not happen—I put the whole question of motherhood on the back burner. Although I would think about it a lot, it was only occasionally that

The Fear would really bubble up. Sometimes a scary headline in a newspaper about declining fertility would do it or someone telling a story of how much someone they knew struggled to get pregnant. Mostly I could push it down, stick my fingers in my ears and say to myself: "La la la la, it's not happening."

On my thirty-fifth birthday in 2019, I launched my newsletter, and for the first six months managed to avoid sharing how I felt about not being a mum. I know a lot of readers assumed I was childfree by choice. I even have friends who thought the same, until I quite publicly announced I was desperate to be a mum, first when I was a guest on Tiffany Philippou's podcast *Totally Fine* and later, in both my newsletter and a *Guardian* article, that was read by half a million people. I wasn't surprised they thought this. I had cultivated a cool-girl persona that gave off the vibe that I didn't care about anything and was having too much fun to worry about kids. Only my best friends knew, and I even found it difficult to talk to them about it. Something that became even harder when, one by one, they edged closer to parenthood.

When the pandemic began, I had a bit of a wake-up call. As a journalist, I was following the news closely, not least because I was one of the reporters manning *The Guardian*'s 24/7 coronavirus liveblog. At the end of January in 2020, on the night the UK left the EU, I interviewed a British guy who had been evacuated from Wuhan, so the virus was on my radar before many of my peers. From what I'd read about when things first got serious in China and then Italy, and then hearing just how long vaccines took to produce, I realized that the pandemic would likely go on for years, and that we could be facing months and months of strict lockdowns.

Just like back on the street outside those drab offices, where I realized it might be hard for me to become a mum, I was hit by another fully formed and terrifying thought: "This could really impact my chances of having a child." I had no evidence to back this thought up, but it was just something I felt to be true. The thought, again, made me catch my breath. There is a phrase, "it weighed heavy on my heart," and that is exactly how it felt—and like a character from a Jane Austen novel, I took to my bed with a cold flannel over my eyes. Dramatic, maybe, but my anxiety was at an all-time high when I had this realization.

It was no longer easy to push The Fear down, and it didn't help that, thanks to the national lockdown, I was bombarded with pictures of happy families everywhere, from Instagram to TV adverts. At the same time, several of my closest friends had their first babies and the friendships that I had come to rely on suddenly went through, understandably, seismic changes. It also brought home to me how much I needed to act if I wanted what they had. Time was—and still is—quite literally running out.

Despite this, I still felt paralyzed by indecision about what to do. I knew I didn't want to try to get into a relationship just to have a baby. That felt wrong to me on so many levels, and I'd also watched people do this and it all go horribly wrong—and yet I also struggled to commit to the idea of going solo.

The Hidden Pain of Social Infertility

During this time, and especially during the third and final lockdown here in the UK, which dragged on for months, The Fear also changed. It had a new flavor, and that flavor was deep sadness. Many people in this position experience what's called ambiguous loss or ambiguous grief. Although it's not the same as how it feels to lose a loved one through death, it is still grieving, and it is very painful and isolating and not discussed enough.

Lori Gottlieb, a psychotherapist and writer, has this to say in an article published in *The Atlantic*, entitled "Dear Therapist: It's Hard to Accept Being Single," that I have shared a few times before:

> In ambiguous grief, there's a murkiness to the loss . . . Ambiguous grief isn't more or less painful than other types of grief—it's just different. But one thing that does make it additionally challenging is that it tends to go unacknowledged. There are no condolence cards

> directed at the person whose spouse is there physically but not cognitively, or the person who can't have the child she dreams of, or the person whose imagined partner has never appeared. There are no community rituals in place to support these people in their grief. They don't get to take a day off work because they're heartbroken that yet another promising date turned out to be a dud and they're back in the throes of ambiguous grief. Instead, their grief goes largely unnoticed.

There is also a term for people like us who don't have children because we are single. The term "social infertility" has been coined by academics to describe those who are unable to have a baby for social reasons, such as not having a partner to try to conceive with. Single women often find it harder to talk about their fertility than those in relationships, and their concerns are often dismissed, whereas women in relationships who are trying for babies or having fertility issues are more likely to elicit sympathy from others. One in five women are childless at midlife, with about 90% of those in that position not so by choice. Being single or not finding the right partner in time accounts for a large majority of those left permanently childless not by choice. Despite this, the subject rarely gets talked about. Headlines screaming about declining fertility blame the fact women are focused on their careers when most women will tell you it's either they haven't found someone they want to procreate with or they just can't afford to have a baby.

When someone is actively trying for a baby and struggling to get pregnant, most people are really sensitive to their feelings, but when someone who really wants to be a mum is single, that doesn't seem to factor in people's heads. People will say "you have plenty of time" in the same breath as talking about time running out for themselves. It's illogical. Actually, those who are single have less time, because we're faced with either trying to find and start a relationship or going down the expensive sperm-donor route. We're already on the back burner.

Not having a baby when you want a baby can impact everything. I have friends who were struggling with fertility who found it difficult to see baby pictures or attend baby showers, and they couldn't be around other people's babies—and usually their mum friends are quite accepting that some find it quite hard, although not always. I don't actually experience this myself. I have almost the opposite problem. I'm so broody that I want to be around babies as much as possible. I recently went to a baby shower and the mother-to-be's brother had brought his five-month-old baby with him. She was so cute and I was desperate for a cuddle. I did not hide it well. As I was hovering near the baby, hungry for a cuddle, like some kind of weirdo, one of my friends, Kate, said to the dad: "I think Nicola would like a baby cuddle." I should probably have been embarrassed that it was so obvious, but instead I was just delighted when he obliged and happily handed the baby over. We chatted while she pulled on my hair and made silly faces, and my heart sang and my arms felt satisfied, as if they had been aching to hold a baby, which, let's face it, they actually are all of the time, in my case.

Another reason why social infertility can be hard is because there is an assumption of blame. It's the idea that you could have been a mum if you had just found yourself a man, so there must be something wrong with you that you couldn't find one to procreate with.

Egg Freezing

Thanks to technology and advances in science, there are some options for women, although clearly none are guaranteed to work. One of them is egg freezing. It has been available in the UK for just over a decade. According to UK fertility regulator, the Human Fertilisation and Embryology Authority (HFEA), the number of women freezing their eggs or embryos rocketed by 523% between 2013 and 2018, and clinics say inquiries rose as much as 50% over lockdown. For my newsletter, I spoke about this with author Sophia Money-Coutts, who had her eggs frozen when she was thirty-five. In her podcast, *Freezing Time*, she shares her audio diaries of the whole process and investigates the science behind egg freezing and its rapid growth in popularity.

I asked her what made her decide to look into egg freezing in the first place, and she told me that soon after she broke up with her ex, a really good girlfriend of hers was having her eggs frozen. Sophia was saddened that her friend had told hardly anyone about it. This would later motivate Sophia to be really open about her experience.

"When she told me, it was because she wanted to ask if I would mind taking her into hospital and picking her up after the operations, because she hadn't even told her mum. She felt she shouldn't talk about it. She was kind of really ashamed about it," Sophia told me. "We both cried, actually, when she came around and she was coming off the anesthetic. She cried, and I cried, and we cried. And we went home and sat down on the sofa; that was the moment I thought, actually, maybe I should start thinking about this, especially as I was newly single. I was around thirty-three then."

Sophia said it took about a year and a half for her to get her head around the idea. "Although I think it can be a very positive decision, for lots of women accepting that this is where you are in your mid-thirties can be hard. It feels like an admission that you're in a place in life where most of your friends probably aren't."

Despite putting herself through the grueling egg-freezing

process, Sophia confessed she wasn't 100% sure she does want to be a mother. She told me: "I still have days when I question if I do really want to be a mum. Sometimes I think I am too selfish and that I do really like my life too much. I do enjoy devoting myself to reading and writing and my work, so I don't know, and maybe that is the answer. If you do want it, maybe you have this burning desire, and if you aren't sure, then you shouldn't? I don't know. These are the questions I'm going to be asking myself over the next few years before I make the decision whether to go for it on my own."

I never really considered egg freezing as an option for me, as the cost is so prohibitive. Most women need at least two if not three cycles to get the number of eggs required, and it can cost between £4,000–£6,000 for each cycle. On top of this, the drugs are around £500–£750 for each cycle, and the cost of keeping the eggs frozen is around £300–£600 a year. Instead I would prefer to go down the solo motherhood route, because if I'm going to have to find such colossal amounts of money, I may as well use it to go the whole hog.

Solo Motherhood by Choice

I don't remember when I first came across Mel Johnson, but she runs a community called The Stork and I for women considering becoming solo mothers by choice, as well as those who already have. For those who don't know, this term—solo mothers—refers to women who have become mothers using a sperm donor. I asked her how she made the decision.

"I split up with my ex, who I thought I would spend the rest of my life with, when I was twenty-nine. I threw myself into dating, but when I was thirty-five I realized that, actually, maybe I'm not going to meet someone and I'm going to have to accept it. At thirty-seven I began to look into my options. It was the realization that I might miss out on motherhood and I had to do something to minimize the chance of missing out. My number-one preference was having a baby with a partner, but I was spending too long on finding one and knew I'd be gutted if I missed out. That's when I decided to go for it because I didn't want to wait anymore."

One of the things I love about Mel is that she shares on social media the realities of solo parenthood and how she copes on a day-to-day basis. As well as battling the fear of never being a mum, the fear of how on earth I would manage it has held me back from making the decision. Back when I was thirty-one and researching this option for the first time, I confidently told my friends that, if I was single at thirty-five, I wouldn't hesitate to have a child on my own. When I actually hit thirty-five, however, I found myself hedging and pushing that "deadline" out further, to thirty-six, thirty-seven, thirty-eight. Partly it's letting go of the way I thought this would go. I always assumed I'd have a partner, a husband even. I thought we would go through it together and that they'd be there, holding my hand through birth and helping share the sleepless nights and the responsibility of decision-making around things like schools, etc.

But there is more to it than that. I'm disorganized. I don't own my own home. I'm freelance, and so my work schedule is all over the place. I've had periods of bad anxiety and depression. I have ADHD. I forget appointments. I'm always late. I'm messy. I'm bad with money. I still get locked out of my house because I forget my keys. Surely all this points to the fact I should only ever become a mother if I've got a supportive and stable partner by my side? Surely I wouldn't be able to do it on my own. One time I voiced these concerns to someone I know, who at the time was a new mum. A married new mum. Her reaction still stings. "Oh, thank God you've said it, because I've been thinking for a while you wouldn't be able to manage it on your own, but didn't want to say," she said. Ouch.

In reality, there are loads of mums out there who are disorganized and often late and they still raise brilliant kids. Some of the things I listed above are also actually outdated beliefs about myself that are no longer true. My house isn't that messy anymore. I've learned to manage my money, and have maintained the highest possible credit rating for years now. I'm also ignoring all the work I've done on myself to manage my mental health and the ways ADHD manifests for me. And by just focusing on the negatives, I'm ignoring all the ways I would be a good mum and what people around me have long known—that I'm really good with kids. I'm also really resourceful, and because I haven't ever really lived with a man, I can do loads of things around the home, like unblock a drain, change lightbulbs, fix the pressure in my boiler and handle really big spiders. I've battled insomnia for years, so I have some experience with lack of sleep. I'm a brilliant multitasker. I live in a great town to raise kids and I also have a brilliant support system around me. My parents would make the world's best grandparents and my sister the best, most fun auntie. I have amazing friends here.

While I've spent the last few years soul-searching about whether I could handle being a single mum, Mel made the decision quickly, as for her it was a no-brainer. She didn't want to end up without a child, so she knew she had to take action. I asked whether she ever doubted that she'd be able to handle it, and she said she didn't.

"I knew having a baby with a sperm donor was a thing, but I didn't know a single thing about it and didn't know anyone else who had done it. I just googled and came across a clinic and called them. I didn't stop to think or worry about how I'd handle it," she says. "As soon as I got pregnant, I was just in total awe at every stage. From choosing maternity clothes to shopping for the baby to having a baby shower to getting my new house ready and nesting, I couldn't believe I was getting to do all those things at last."

The awe didn't stop when the baby—Daisy, who is now in infant school—arrived. "I remember the first walk I went on with her and I was thinking, 'Oh my God, I'm pushing a pram and it's my baby inside.' I was just so in awe that I didn't stop to panic or worry about doing it alone."

Hearing Mel speak makes me want to run straight to the nearest fertility clinic. But then I remember how much it is going to cost. Not only would I have to afford treatment—potentially IVF, which is not often offered to single women on the NHS—but I would also need to save for actually having a baby, as my parent friends are always telling me how expensive they are, which, added to the fact I'm self-employed and would only get statutory maternity pay, which is very low, it sometimes feels like an impossible feat. I also want to buy a house before I try to have a baby, and that's difficult enough on one's own.

That brings me back to thinking it would be more feasible to wait to find a partner and try with them, but bringing up a baby with a partner has its own challenges and drawbacks. For the last few years, as I have considered what to do, I have often found myself reading articles and books and Instagram posts by mothers in heterosexual relationships about their experience. I am so glad this work exists, and it's great that so many women are talking so openly about the challenges and disparities that exist, but—and I say this with utmost respect—they aren't really selling the whole marriage/live-in boyfriend thing to me. In fact, they are actively putting me off. So many of the posts deal with how men still aren't pulling their weight when it comes to housework and childcare, as well as the mental load and emotional labor women have to do that their male partners don't do. This resentment festers and you can tell that, beneath the funny memes, there is a well of rage. If this is what long-term relationships and marriage look like, I'd rather go it alone, I often think. Of course I know there are benefits to long-term love, but it is so depressing that it's still like this. My sister often finds comfort in single life if she is ever feeling low by reading forums on Mumsnet, where hundreds of women vent about their husbands not helping with the kids or around the house.

Fertility Checks

I know I will regret it if I don't at least begin to explore my options, instead of remaining in this decision-paralysis. I've been thinking of going to a fertility clinic and getting tested to see what they say. An AMH test, for example, measures levels of anti-mullerian hormone, which corresponds to a person's egg count. This test and others can give you an idea of your fertility timeline, which can help you think about your next steps.

It was actually a fertility test that led Genevieve Roberts, author of *Going Solo*, to decide to have her first baby girl on her own. She later had a little boy using the same donor, and has recently had a baby with her now-husband, who she met when she was a single mother. I interviewed her for my newsletter in 2020, when she was still single, and she told me about what led her to make the decision to go for it on her own.

> I'd had a miscarriage a couple of years previously. After some time, I got over the relationship, which ended shortly after it. But when I was pregnant, it wasn't just that I'd imagined the future with a child, it was that I had mentally made all the sacrifices and decisions and I felt very fulfilled at the idea of it. I came to terms with losing the boyfriend and I got over that, but the idea of being a parent didn't really go away.

She decided to get her fertility tested a few years later.

> I expected it to be high, that children would be woven into my future and I could just carry on with dating. But it came out very, very low. I was told that if I wanted to have children, I should try right away but there was no guarantee. I was actually told IVF might

> be the only way to conceive. I think [having the fertility test] was a good call as it did sharpen my mind and make me think about what I really wanted.

Aside from the financial worries and where I would live with a baby, one worry I used to have that I know some readers still do have, is what the reactions of others will be like. I asked Genevieve what her loved ones said when she announced her plans. She told me that everyone was supportive and offered to help in any way they could. It was only her mum, although also very supportive, who expressed some worries to her.

> My mum said to me that she had concerns that I was choosing a hard life for myself and that I would always be her child: she wanted an easy life for me. I really understood that and think it was a really nice thing to say, but I just explained that not having a child wasn't easy either.
>
> I think it's really hard for people on the outside to understand when they see someone with a fulfilling career, who works hard and who is always jetting off to all sorts of places. Those things were amazing and they were fulfilling, but just for me—and it's different for everyone—I really wanted to become a parent as well.

I also sometimes worry about depriving a child of a father, especially as I've always been such a daddy's girl, and whether they'd be damaged by the idea of not knowing much about where they came from on that side. But from what I have learned, I know that the best way to handle this is to be as honest and straightforward as possible from day one. Problems are more likely to occur when children are lied to or think someone else is their biological dad. Donor-conceived children also say they prefer to have a donor who is happy to be contacted rather than an anonymous one.

I asked Liv Thorne, author of *Liv's Alone*, about this. She said: "Herb doesn't know what it's like to have a dad. No one's walked out on him. No one's died on him. Whether that's good or bad, I don't know. But these are the facts of his life and he knows all about it and he talks about it all the time. I've always been very honest with him. Occasionally he'll say he is sad because he would like to have a brother, but he'd never said he is sad not to have a dad or granddad."

Other Options

Buying sperm from a sperm bank is not the only way to become a mother. You could choose a known donor instead of an anonymous sperm donor, which means your child will have more information about their father—although this opens up the possibility of the donor wanting more contact or even shared custody, and it can be risky because, unlike with a sperm bank, there wouldn't be any testing, etc., but I can understand why some women feel it is their only option if they can't afford to go the more legitimate route.

Another option, which is fairly common in the queer community and which I think is really cool, is choosing to have a baby with a friend (or even a stranger—there are actually apps to help you find someone) and platonically co-parenting together. I first heard about this concept around five years ago, after making friends with a woman while doing jury duty. She and her wife were raising two awesome children with a single gay man. Originally they had asked him to be a known donor, but he came back and said that, actually, he wanted to be a dad. The children don't just have the love of a father, as well as their two mothers, but also all of the extended family members.

I loved this story and thought the children were so lucky. I also love the way this route shakes up the status quo. Unlike being forced into sharing custody after the breakdown of a relationship, they were choosing to very consciously co-parent from the start. I always get emotional when I hear stories like that of my friends. It also really appeals to me as an option, but obviously, finding the right person who you can see yourself parenting a child with for the rest of your lives is a bit of a challenge.

What If It Never Happens?

It's also important to consider, no matter how hard it may feel, the fact that I may end up involuntarily childless. For a long time I refused to even let myself think about this and wouldn't read anything about how it feels because I was too afraid. But after a while I realized I should face the issue head on.

In a post on *Grief Is the Word*, an anonymous blog by a childless woman that I came across in my research, the author writes about what ambiguous grief feels like, and that you have a right to feel as if you are grieving. She says: "If you are grieving the nonexistence of something or the potential nonexistence of something, there is often no death date, no start date before which you were not grieving, and after which you began to grieve. Hope may diminish so gradually as to be imperceptible, so you may not even know when your grief began. When does anticipatory grief become grief of something 'actual'? Only you can decide the end point of your own hope."

I also spoke to Jody Day, author of *Living the Life Unexpected* and founder of Gateway Women, the community of childless women that I mentioned in an earlier chapter. Jody's story is a hard one to hear if, like me, you are still hoping motherhood is in your future, but I'm really glad I took the time to listen and to hear how she has built a fulfilled and meaningful life for herself since she had the realization that she wouldn't ever be a mother.

Talking to Jody has also clarified things for me. While it didn't end up how she expected, she did try really hard to have a baby, whereas I have been floundering in my indecision for the best part of a decade and haven't tried at all. I know I will regret it, and my grief will be worse, if I don't take action.

She remembers the moment she realized vividly. She was forty-four, divorced, and the five-year relationship that began after her marriage ended was also over. In both relationships, she had been trying for a baby. After the relationship ended, she was staring out of the window in her Notting Hill studio flat when she suddenly knew with complete certainty that she'd never have a baby.

"I just thought, that's it. I'm never, ever going to be a mother. An incredible calm came over me. It was one of those moments in your life where you can really remember yourself back into it."

At first she felt relief, which surprised her.

"There was this part of me, which was the part that for fifteen years had been hoping, planning, trying, thinking, nesting and everything was all on this eventual motherhood trajectory. Then this other part of me, which felt like a path of energy, was actually the life I'd actually been living, the person I actually was and the things I'd actually been doing. There was a sense of these two halves of me coming back together for the first time."

She went to make herself a cup of tea and thought back to when she was twenty, and she had felt like she'd be able to achieve anything she put her mind to.

"I thought to myself in that moment, 'Well, why can't the years from forty-five to seventy-five feel like that? Why can't I imagine a great life for myself again?' That feeling lasted for a couple of hours and I'm really grateful for that, because after that I fell into a pit of despair. It felt like that scene in *Trainspotting* where the guy disappears into the carpet. It was the most profound despair I've ever experienced and I've had a lot of difficult experiences in my life. But this despair didn't lift."

Jody says that for two years she "floundered" around in her despair and tried to seek help. Nobody could tell her what it was other than depression, which wasn't quite right. It was only when she was studying grief models while training to become a psychotherapist that she realized.

"I went home that evening, and I mapped out the experience with the model I was learning against my internal reality, and that was the first time I was like, 'Oh my God, I'm grieving.' Those two years were incredibly hard. No one would let me talk about it. I withdrew from my friends. It was incredibly, intensely lonely and painful."

With no one to turn to, Jody began writing about her experience. She started a blog and was also interviewed for the national press. Soon she was inundated with messages from other people like her. She realized she wasn't alone and that many people needed support, so she launched Gateway Women soon after. Turning something so painful into something so positive has been a powerful experience.

"To those people who see those who don't have children as somehow emotionally immature, I would say that not becoming a mother, when I wanted to be one, has had as profound an impact on me and on the course of my life and my development as a person as being a mother would have done, just in a completely different way," she says. "There's the Jody who would have been a mum, and that would have been a messy, imperfect experience, and there's the Jody who isn't a mum, and it's also a messy, imperfect experience. One is not more valuable than the other."

I agree with Jody. Even though I want to be a mum and am still hoping it will happen for me, I find it hard to be treated like my life matters less because I don't have kids. I hope that, if it does happen for me, I can hang on to what that feels like and make sure I don't make anyone else feel that way.

ELEVEN
The D Word

Readers of my newsletter will know that I rarely mention dating when I write about single life. It's not that I don't think it's an important part of the single experience or that I disapprove or hate romance, it's simply that dating dominates almost every other conversation when it comes to talking about being single. I wanted to create a space that was free from that, so that people could discuss all the other parts of being single that get overlooked. It also feels a little rebellious to leave dating out of the conversation when so many people assume that, if I write about being single, then it must be that what I actually write about is dating. A lot of people actually assume I'm a dating columnist when they first hear what I do.

I've had countless conversations since I first began to write about being unattached that prove my point. Recently I bumped into a neighbor, who asked what I was working on, and when I told him about the book, he replied that he had missed "the whole dating thing" because he'd met his wife so young. He looked completely blank when I explained that, actually, I was writing about the vast kaleidoscope of experience that single people have.

As I've mentioned before, one of the reasons it annoys me is that it feels like it is only acceptable to be single if you are actively trying not to be—and for vast periods of my near decade of singleness, I haven't actually been actively looking for a romantic partner on dating apps or elsewhere. I just haven't felt like it. Endless swiping and text conversations with strangers just isn't how I want to spend my one wild and precious life.

In fact, I've never actually been on a date off the back of a dating app. Yes, you read that right. Given I lived in London for seven years, where it almost feels sacrilegious to admit such a thing, and it usually really surprises people. I know this makes me an outlier as a single millennial. It feels like dating apps are almost a rite of passage and I'm somehow doing single life wrong for not having a raft of dating-app horror stories to entertain my coupled-up friends with.

But all of my former relationships, dates, flings and flirtations have actually been with people I met in real life, either as we were already friends, we worked together, or I was introduced by another friend, or we met on a night out. Maybe that makes me old-fashioned, but that's just how it's always been for me. As already mentioned, there have also been long periods where I wasn't looking at all and was just enjoying being on my own.

Every once in a while, like back in October 2021, I'll redownload the apps and, usually, after an initial feeling of fun, I'll soon become jaded and pissed off. Invariably some arsehole will say something annoying or misogynistic (or usually both). One time, a guy I was due to actually meet in real life called me a "greedy bint" because I told him I'd seen two separate sets of friends that evening (which was actually thanks to me double-booking myself!). Another time, I'd been chatting to someone I thought was really lovely, but when I didn't go on the app for a couple of days as I was away visiting friends, he took it personally, and when I next went on to message him, I received a long paragraph of a message detailing what a bitch I was for ghosting him when he thought we had a connection. I was blocked before I had a chance to explain that, actually, I just hadn't opened the app for two days.

The older I've gotten, and the more concerned I've become about my fertility declining, the more I have been turned off by the idea of dating. It feels so awkward and forced and I always wonder when it would be appropriate to bring up that I want children—and that I'm going to need to start trying fairly soon because of my age. Because the problem of wanting to be a mother is at the forefront of every decision I make, I feel like I'd just be hunting for a man to procreate with rather than really clearly considering if they are actually the right guy for me long term, children or no children. It's a bit like the advice not to go to the supermarket when you're hungry because you'll end up buying a bunch of stuff you don't need. Dating when you are longing to start trying for a baby feels like a recipe for disaster, although I know plenty of people do meet The One in their late thirties and early forties and go on to have children and it all works out beautifully. For me, it just feels too risky, especially as I feel so comfortable being on my own—and because of various negative stories I've heard from friends and friends of friends stuck parenting with someone they really wish they weren't.

What's Wrong with Modern Dating?

Dating apps do not make me feel good, and yet conventional dating wisdom says that, to find a partner, we need to treat dating like a job and dedicate time and energy to it. Frankly, I have better things to do. Once in a while, however, someone will contact me for advice. They'll complain that dating apps are sucking the joy from their soul but say they don't know how else to meet someone and so they feel trapped on them. Often these women will mention they want to have children.

Given my aversion to dating apps, I'm definitely not the best person to ask, but it's a common problem, so I spoke to *Vogue*'s dating columnist, Annie Lord, who I'd spoken to previously about heartbreak. I wanted to know if I was just being cynical, or was modern dating really awful.

"No, it is awful," she says. "I think it's a combination of things. The flakiness does go both ways, but I think a lot of the time it is more on the men's side. I think a lot of men just see it as a game, so they chat to you for ages and then nothing happens. I think that's because, once men see it is progressing and they know they could have sex, they can't even be bothered to go through with it because they feel like they've won the game already, whereas I think women actually just want to have sex."

Annie thinks a lot of people are also putting more emphasis on other areas of their life, including their work and friends. Going on a date when so often they end up going nowhere can feel like wasted time. "I don't know many people now that would choose to go out with a stranger rather than go to the pub with their whole friend group. I really see a lot of people prioritizing their friends now, which is nice, but can be annoying when you're trying to organize a date.

"I don't even want a boyfriend right now, but I'm just bored. The dating apps just feel really stagnant," Annie says. "My friend sent me something today that made me laugh. She said: 'I think the man crisis is like the housing crisis. All the good ones are in long-term contracts and we're just left with the shoddy new builds that fall apart as soon as you put up a sideboard.'"

Podcast host and writer Shani Silver, author of *A Single Revolution*, advocates for ditching dating apps altogether if they are making you miserable. As she says in her book, dating apps are designed to keep you on them, and designed to encourage you to re-download them again if you do manage to break free for a short time. That's how the companies that run them make their money—by making you feel like you need them and that there is absolutely no other way to meet someone.

Despite the claims of all the dating apps and what many people assume, they really aren't the only way to meet someone. I know this for a fact because, one day, I decided to ask Twitter/X for people who hadn't met their partner on a dating app to tell me how their "meet cute" had happened. I said I particularly wanted recent stories. Within hours I was overwhelmed with hundreds of accounts. People had met their partners at life-drawing classes, through a meet-up group for walkers, at a Halloween party, when selling their car, when renting out a room in their house, while singing in a band, on a work training course, while white-water rafting, on the dance floor, in a club, down the pub, and even on Twitter/X.

I spoke to Shani for my newsletter and raised the fact that some people had told me they were too scared to delete their dating apps even though they hated them. Shani pointed out to me that it might be helpful to reframe the problem and for people to evaluate why they want a partner so badly in the first place.

She told me:

> What exactly do you think it's going to do for you, and is that actually worth feeling bad because you don't have it or have trouble finding it? To me this suggests a sense of incompleteness, and we are simply not incomplete. Next, I think when you feel compelled to use dating apps or you'll "never find someone," you've started viewing life through a very small window, and dating apps are great at making you think they're your only option, no matter how many years you spend using them to no avail.
>
> We live in a world much larger than what exists on our phone, and sometimes you have to take a step back and remind yourself that you deserve so much more than swiping your adulthood away.

How to Have a More Positive Dating-App Experience

For those who are dating and are okay about being on the apps, perhaps there are ways to ensure your experience is more positive than negative? I asked Jillian Anthony, host of the *Cruel Summer Book Club* podcast and former lead editor of *Time Out New York*, about her experience of dating.

After going through a breakup and being made redundant in New York, she planned to head to Europe to travel for six months in 2020, but the pandemic put paid to that. Instead she set off on a solo road trip across the US, stopping to hike in America's stunning national parks, and used Tinder wherever she went. After the adventure, she decided to move to Austin, Texas.

"It was some of the best dating I've ever done. I think it was that there was this container, where we knew it could go nowhere. The pressure was off. When I moved to Austin, I went wild dating and had so much fun. I called it my 'tits-out summer.' It was a very flirty and fun summer and it was great."

After her "tits-out summer," Jillian decided she would spend a year taking dating more seriously and doing it more intentionally than she did before. She has shifted the approach she took when she was younger and is now centering herself in all dating situations. In an edition of her newsletter, she wrote:

> Most of my dating life, I wondered and worried about what the men I was interested in thought about me. "Does he think I'm hot, smart, cool, funny? Does he

> like me? Does he want to see me again? Is he thinking about me? Will he call? Does he want to be my boyfriend?"
>
> Their approval of me was all that mattered; never mind if I was genuinely interested in them, or if they added value to my life. A lifetime of growing up as an American girl taught me to view myself through the exacting sightline of the male gaze. I gave all of my power over to the opinions of strangers I barely knew. My peace and happiness rested on their approval and desire of me, though few of them ever earned the right to that sort of respect and personal influence.

Jillian told me:

> It shouldn't matter whether he likes me for a while. At first, it should all be about whether I feel good when I'm in their presence. That's how I've changed things. I think most dating advice is total bullshit. I'm still unlearning so much as I'm aging about what as a woman I should be doing by now and those messages are very intense in the dating world.

In an agony aunt column for her *Tough Love* newsletter on Substack, Tiffany Philippou points out that the apps are designed to give you the same addictive dopamine hits as the likes of betting and social media companies.

The trick to beating the game, she argues, is to separate

ourselves and our worth from our dating profiles. The apps, she says, should be seen as simply a tool to help you meet more people in the world. If you get bad vibes or someone doesn't arrange to meet in real life, don't waste your time. Simply tap out of that conversation and keep going. She writes that all people should be looking for at the initial stage of being on the apps is someone to meet and have a nice conversation with—and instead of thinking that you must find The One, see it as an opportunity to have a little flirt with someone.

"Don't get validation from likes and matches, just as anyone disappearing, unmatching or not liking you back shouldn't make you insecure," she says. "You are so much more than a handful of photos and answers to prompts, so don't become attached to how someone responds to those things. The highs and lows and ego-validatory dopamine hits don't serve your purpose. Save the ego massaging for when you're flirting with someone IRL."

Sex and the Single Woman

Of course, dating is also about finding people to have sex with. There is a lot of evidence that sex is seriously good for our mental and physical health. It lowers the heart rate and blood pressure, reducing our risk of heart disease. It boosts the immune system to protect us against infections and it certainly lowers stress, thanks to oxytocin, the hormone released after sex. The NHS even recommends it. Hidden away on its website, it advises: "Weekly sex might help fend off illness."

For those who don't want to date, but don't want to be celibate, there's obviously the prospect of casual sex or having a "friends with benefits" agreement. A member of my Facebook community told me about her "fuck buddy" and how it works for her. She said the setup had made her love her single life more, because she was able to have regular good sex with someone she felt completely safe and comfortable with, as opposed to having one-night stands, which can feel more risky. This is definitely something I struggle with. Shagging a stranger can be fun, but it's also a vulnerable position to be in. Sometimes it can even be scary.

In Katherine Angel's *Tomorrow Sex Will Be Good Again*, a nonfiction book about the politics of desire, she writes that women are in a bind. In the name of sexual consent and feminist empowerment, we are told we must proclaim our desires clearly and confidently, but sex researchers tell us that women don't know what we want. And men are on hand to persuade heterosexual women that what they want is, in fact, exactly what men want.

As many women have had uncomfortable sexual experiences or even experienced sexual assault and violence, the idea of a one-night stand or even sex with someone you're just starting to see can be nerve-wracking and even triggering. There is also the fact that sex, even with someone you trust, requires vulnerability.

"For many women, life—and sex—are a complex tussle between the need to harden, fortify, and push away on the one hand, and the need to receive, dissolve and allow on the other," Katherine writes. "Women especially know the vulnerability which reigns over their lives—they are made to know this, painfully, forcefully, too often, whether in the form of actual violation and invasion, or in the constant reminders of it."

Feeling Sexy and Confident When Single

There are other reasons it can be hard to relax. Becoming comfortable having sex and learning what you actually like is something comedian Sadia Azmat has explored in her book, *Sex Bomb*, and while being single. She says she wrote her book for people who don't really fit into the standard dating scene, where she is often fetishized, or in the Muslim arranged marriage scene, where, in her words, "people think even eye contact is too much."

Sadia, who is the host of critically acclaimed BBC podcast *No Country for Young Women*, argues that women aren't either nuns or whores, but that women are raised to please, which is why heterosexual women don't always enjoy sex as much. If you can find someone to be vulnerable and honest with, whether that is a friend with benefits or other setup, it can help you explore your sexuality outside of a committed relationship.

"I thought a big part of my role was to please the man. I think as soon as I stopped putting that on myself and started to not worry about the man or what he thought of me and just being free, I definitely felt sexier," she says.

She would love for more people to be able to feel that way and to be able to talk more openly about sex, whether they are in a relationship or not. "As a Muslim woman, it's not like one day I woke up and thought 'I'm fucking sexy.' I had a lot of layers to get through—and I don't just mean in terms of clothing—and a lot of things to unlearn," she says. "I actually think learning to be more vulnerable and honest made the biggest difference and that is something I learned when I became a stand-up comedian, because you have to be so honest. And when you're on stage, you're vulnerable and feel almost naked."

There may also be periods in your life when you feel much more confident and sexy than others. One of the last times I hooked up with someone was at my friend's wedding. It was in the sunny Cotswolds and it was festival-themed. It was a great wedding. My friend Mel, who I've known since I was nineteen, when we were both working at a rock club in Leicester while at university, had kindly arranged for me and a few other single girls, some of whom I'd met on the hen do, to share a yurt, and a number of other university friends were also in attendance, two of whom had chosen not to bring their husbands. Kids weren't invited, so the mums and dads in attendance, free from the obligations of caring for little ones, were in very high spirits. It was basically the opposite of a single woman's worst wedding nightmare.

The day got better when the bride pulled me aside and said, if I was interested, she would tell me which of the guys were single. I was feeling good about myself and in the mood for some fun, so I paid attention as she pointed each of them out. Later, one of the single guys sidled up to me. (I haven't asked, but I wonder if the groom had also pointed out the single women to him.) The man in question had a big wide smile and huge sparkly blue eyes. After dancing and laughing for a while, we were soon giving Kourtney Kardashian and Travis Barker a run for their money when it came to packing on the PDA. It was like we were teenagers. We were snogging and grinding against each other on the dance floor with abandon, to the point where we were actually turning heads. After a while, we told everyone we were "going for a walk," which obviously none of them were fooled by. Our walk took us to his yurt.

The next morning the bride came over to congratulate me on my conquest and joked that I seemed to have a good track record at events she has organized, because I also happened to have scored at her hen do, which had been in Croatia a couple of months beforehand. I laughed, and cringed slightly, wondering what on earth her friends must have thought of me, but it was all harmless fun. All in all, it had been a good summer. I was in the period of my life where I felt most happy to be single and I also felt confident and sexy. It's probably not a coincidence that, not long after, high on this great summer, I began writing publicly about single life.

Six months later, the pandemic hit and I ended up moving home with my parents for the first lockdown, and then, later, into a house on my own for the second and third lockdowns. I decided to follow the Covid rules as much as possible, as my dad was quite high risk, and so I wasn't one of those to enjoy an illicit lockdown love affair. I was unintentionally celibate but okay about it.

Years before, during another dry spell, I had been deeply ashamed and even quite depressed about it. But in the pandemic, I honestly didn't worry too much about it. Maybe that's getting older for you? Maybe I just had other concerns that felt more important to me? Maybe it's because I'd invested in a much better vibrator?

I actually forgot how long it had been since I'd enjoyed a proper kiss, let alone anything more, until I met up with Mel for lunch in Birmingham after the last lockdown was lifted and met her baby for the first time. While the baby napped, we reminisced about the wedding and hen do and also what I got up to on both. I dropped in that her wedding was the last time I'd had any action. "Oh my God," she said, jaw dropping. "You need to get on that." I laughed and asked if she could please organize another event for my benefit.

Even as I said it, I thought things would probably have been different if the hen do and wedding had been happening that year instead. Thanks to a combination of spending so much enforced time alone, body image woes and mental health dips, I had lost all that sparkly confidence I'd had in 2019. It was holding me back from—to use the dreaded phrase—"putting myself out there." I felt closed off, like the pandemic had somehow shut that door in me. It wasn't a libido thing; it was feeling like I didn't know how to be charming and flirty and sexy anymore. I felt awkward and self-conscious. I thought back to that girl who had had so much fun that summer and she felt like a stranger.

Touch Deprivation

One thing I had noticed during that period, which I think impacted how I felt, was that, as time went on, especially during the last lockdown, which in the UK dragged on for five months, my body was craving touch. It wasn't just the sexy kind of touch, though. I was also missing those little everyday tactile moments, when someone taps your arm or kisses your cheek or rests their hand on your shoulder. They soon add up. It was only when things began to return to normal and this kind of casual touching was back on the cards again that I realized how much I had been impacted by touch deprivation.

One time, in a shop, I accidentally grazed fingers with the assistant as I went to pack my bag. It felt like an electric shock shooting through my body. For hours after I could feel the place where we had touched. Another time, as restrictions were easing, a friend lightly stroked my back when asking what I wanted from the bar while we were sitting in a beer garden. I was so sensitive that my skin felt warm and tingly on the spot she had touched and the feeling seemed to spread over my whole body. I wanted and needed more.

Researchers point to the massive impact touch can have, which goes to show it wasn't all in my head. Tiffany Field, director of the Touch Research Institute at the University of Miami Miller School of Medicine, wrote in an article for *The Guardian* that, like diet and exercise, everyone needs a daily dose of touch, and when we are starved of that, as many single people are, it can have huge impacts on our health and well-being. Tiffany explains why this is: "Touch calms the nervous system, lowers blood pressure as well as stress hormones, which in turn means that immune cells can survive . . . We can also experience less pain and depression as the body's natural pain killer, serotonin, is also its natural antidepressant."

On my birthday in October 2021, I decided to book in for a massage and a facial during a spa day that I had been dreaming about since the start of the pandemic. The massage was brilliant but—and this surprised me—it wasn't until the facial that I felt like crying. There was something about having my face caressed that made me feel less alone somehow. I realized that touching someone's face is actually quite an intimate thing to do. It's not something that happens on an everyday basis, especially if you are single.

There was another reason it made me emotional. It reminded me of my most significant ex-boyfriend, James. When he'd have his arm around me, he would lightly tap my cheeks to show affection or sometimes to annoy me. It wasn't that I wanted him to stroke my face again; I just missed that intimacy. That physical language couples share with each other. I wondered when a man would next hold my face and kiss me. It made me think that I needed to get back to 2019 Nicola—or even perhaps 2010 Nicola—when I had been someone who was regularly touched and held. I realized how much I missed it. But it also made me feel nervous. Maybe I wouldn't remember how to do it after all this time on my own? In the end, thanks to a drunken encounter with an old friend, I only had to wait a couple more weeks before someone held my face and snogged me. Turns out, it's just like riding a bike.

Helping Yourself

Going for a massage or even learning self-massage technique can help with touch deprivation, but there are other things you can do too, such as getting your nails done or something else equally pampering, buying a weighted blanket, spending quality time with animals or learning to dance or trying acro-yoga. There are even things called cuddle parties, which are events where consensual platonic touch is practiced. These things can help, but, for me at least, they just don't replace the real thing.

Of course there are other things we can do by ourselves. Masturbation, still so often talked about in hushed tones or portrayed as simply a turn-on for the male gaze, is actually really healthy and can boost your mental wellbeing. Instead of being something shameful, it is increasingly something people include in their self-care routines. Despite this, there is a "masturbation gap." In 2023, Lovehoney found that while men reported masturbating around 191 times a year, women, on average, only masturbated around seventy times a year. Lovehoney's sex and relationships expert, Annabelle Knight, has said one of the primary reasons for the gap is that "there is still a stigma and taboo around female masturbation, where the same doesn't exist for males."

Perhaps it's also because, as comedian Sadia Azmat says about sex, heterosexual women don't enjoy it as much, as they aren't actually sure what they like, as we have always been conditioned to please men. The website OMGYES .com is a good place to start if you're interested in getting better at it. It aims to "demystify" female pleasure through education and instruction. There are video demonstrations and even a touch-screen tutorial, where users can practice and improve their own technique.

Investing in some good sex toys is another way, of course. Once a seedy product advertised in the back of porno magazines, vibrators and dildos, etc. are now commonplace additions to nightstands up and down the country—and it's women who have driven the change. Erica Braverman, whose dad, Ron, co-founded sex toy company Doc Johnson in 1976, told the BBC that "the imagery and the perception of sex toys has changed completely." A famous scene in *Sex and the City*, where the four main characters are sitting around discussing a vibrator, was a "huge moment" for the industry, Erica told the BBC. "Feminism comes into play a lot," she said. "I think empowering women has been a big reason why this industry has been pushed forward so much in recent years."

A lot of articles about sex toys still refer to use by couples, but according to Business Wire, the adoption and use of sex toys is growing, especially among single women, for people wanting to masturbate solo with sex toys, such as vibrators, clitoral stimulators/suction vibrators and internal vaginal toys among others. There are now so many options on the market, and many of them are marketed as luxury goods and part of the wellness industry.

Some women pair sex toys with porn, and there are also many sites that offer an experience tailored to getting women off while being as ethical as possible to those taking part. This is something feminist filmmaker Erika Lust advocates for in her 2014 TEDx talk "It's Time for Porn to Change." Dissatisfied with the portrayal of women in the mainstream adult industry, where the focus remains on male pleasure, Erika began making explicit films and then launched Lust Cinema, where you can watch porn videos, many made by female directors, showing "intimacy, love, and lust in sex," where "the feminine POV is vital, the aesthetic is a pleasure to all of the senses, and eroticism and innovation are celebrated." For those who are single and queer, CrashPad (https://crashpadseries.com) is an award-winning porn site that provides "real dyke porn, lesbians, femme on femme, boi, stud, genderqueer and trans-masculine performers, transwomen, transmen, queer men and women engaging in authentic queer sexuality."

The resurgence in popularity of erotica and, more recently, audio porn aimed at women points to things beginning to shift. For those who want to give the latter a try, BLOOM (https://www.bloomstories.com) features a diverse range of audio erotic content, encompassing fictional narratives across various genres, notably featuring a comprehensive catalog centered on queer experiences. Additionally, the platform offers guided masturbation sessions and ASMR porn. Sssh.com, a recognized ethical porn platform, meanwhile, focuses on sex-positive erotic content presented from a woman's point of view.

Is Ethical Non-Monogamy the Answer?

For those who want intimacy and physical contact, there is also another way, if traditional dating doesn't appeal. Ethical non-monogamy is becoming more common and one person I interviewed told me about how she considers herself single, although she has what she calls a part-time boyfriend. He is married and in an open relationship. It suits her, she said, because she can go on fun dates with him and have good sex, but she still gets to enjoy her house to herself and doesn't have to deal with any domesticity.

Another told me about how going to women-only sex parties in London had given her a way to explore her sexuality in a safe way without anyone's feelings getting hurt, and in a place where communicating boundaries, as well as wants and desires, is encouraged.

Writer Cathy Reay says she fell into polyamory accidentally when she started dating someone who was polyamorous. Cathy, a mum of two, was previously in a heterosexual monogamous marriage. When she began dating after her divorce, polyamory was not on her radar.

"I—like everyone else—grew up in a very mono-normative world, so I didn't know much about polyamory. I just kind of assumed, as I think a lot of people do, that it was for people who wanted to casually date without a lot of commitment, which is absolutely fine if that's what you want to do, but it wasn't what I wanted to do."

After reading up on it and talking to other people, she realized that polyamorous relationships take many shapes and forms (for example, many polyamorous people are married, cohabiting or raising kids together). She felt excited about shaping the narrative of her relationships to suit her, and not just following the traditional relationship pattern.

"I decided to give it a go and see if I got jealous. It didn't work out between me and that guy, but being with him gave me an avenue to explore polyamory for myself, and this soon helped me to realize that I wasn't heterosexual after all."

Cathy says dating in this way fits in perfectly with being a busy working single mum, as no one she dates has unrealistic expectations about her available time, as is sometimes the case in more traditional relationships.

"I'm just honest about the time I have and really clear on what I can do and what my expectations are, and then try to find people that match with that," Cathy says. "It's actually been easier, in a way, because before, when I used to date straight guys, I would just fall head over heels with them and they consumed my whole life and I'd be quite co-dependent in that scenario, typically wanting to rescue them or whatever, even if they didn't need to be rescued. And painting an unrealistic picture of what the future might look like without ever actually having that conversation. In polyamory, I talk lots to people I'm dating about logistics and expectations—and that, for me, is so much more freeing, because we both know exactly where we stand."

This type of dating isn't just for younger people. In November 2022, Feeld, an app for people interested in casual sex, polyamory, kink, swinging and other alternative sexual preferences, hit the headlines. The app has been popular with millennials since its launch in 2014, but according to the app's founders, midlifers are the fastest-rising demographic among its users. In fact, the numbers of over-fifties more than doubled between

October 2021 and 2022. *The Times* has called this the midlife sexual revolution.

One user, a fifty-one-year-old single woman, told *The Times* that, after coming out of a fifteen-year marriage, she wanted to join the site to explore. She said: "I am still really fit, my body is good, I really enjoy sex and wanted to experiment. Sex isn't something I want to go without or feel guilty about. The challenge before was finding an emotionally healthy scenario in which to do it."

How I Feel About Dating Going Forward

Although I still feel very resistant to the idea of domesticity, which is one of the things holding me back from dating, talking to all these amazing women has given me food for thought about the alternatives. I have also realized that, probably because I'm so focused on how I'll have a baby and yet I don't wish to date to find a man to procreate with, I have closed myself off from all kinds of dating—even the type that is just for fun.

The conversations I've had for this chapter have actually made me feel a little bit like I've accidentally turned into a nun these last few years. It's partly about body confidence—I'm ashamed to admit that I often catch myself thinking that "I'll put myself out there again when I've lost X number of pounds," and it's hard to shake that mindset even though, intellectually, I know that my size doesn't matter—and that all bodies can be sexy.

My reticence is also about not feeling my old sparkly confident self in general. I feel like I've forgotten how to flirt—even though flirting is one of my favorite things. I am blaming the pandemic for that. But the pandemic has been over for a while now. Maybe it's time for my own "tits-out summer"?

TWELVE

Saying Goodbye to Our Single Identity

The first question most people ask me when they discover what I write about is this: "What will you do when you get a boyfriend?" The question always makes me smile, because it just goes to show that everyone assumes being single is a waiting room that you'll eventually leave. But I guess the other reason people wonder about this is because, thanks to my newsletter, the articles I've written for the national press, and the appearances I've made on national radio, being single has a lot to do with who I am and what I do for a living. In short, it's become a big part of my identity.

While making a career out of their relationship status isn't that common, lots of people nevertheless feel defined by their single status. As I have hopefully shown throughout these pages, there are many reasons to feel proud of being single. Many of the people I've written about in this book love being on their own. But none of us know what is round the corner. Some of us may well end up leaving our single era behind us and getting into a relationship.

About a year ago a member of the Facebook group I run posted a goodbye message. She had met someone unexpectedly and was leaving the group as she didn't feel like she should stay when she wasn't single. "I twice considered leaving the group without saying goodbye. But I couldn't," the post began. It was emotional. She thanked everyone for their support and said the community had meant the world to her during a period when she really needed it (the pandemic was still in full force). Another time I had an email from a reader telling me she had found someone and would be unsubscribing. It was such a sweet message. Both seemed to feel a little sheepish about their news and both were feeling emotional about leaving the community.

Not long after, my friend Tiffany Philippou told me she had some news to share. We were making the most of freelance life by having a pint one midweek afternoon in a London pub. "I've got something to tell you," she said. "I'm leaving the single community." She then proceeded to tell me that she'd formalized things with the guy she'd been seeing for a while. I knew she had been seeing him, so the news didn't come as a shock, but I was a little surprised and also touched at the way she told me. We talked about how she felt like she was losing her single identity. She went on to write about these complicated feelings for her newsletter, *The Tiff Weekly*, and for the *i* paper.

I asked Tiffany, who is the author of *Totally Fine (And Other Lies I've Told Myself)*, what was going through her mind when she shared her announcement with me. She told me: "I wasn't fully aware that I had a single identity until I was stepping outside of it and, when I was confronted with the reality of entering a relationship, and almost like taking that leap, it felt like a loss."

This took her a bit by surprise, as she'd been the one pushing for a proper relationship, while her boyfriend wasn't so sure about committing, as he'd just come out of a long-term relationship. "Being with someone that wasn't actually ready to commit was also a bit of a safety net too, for me. When I was faced with the reality of it, all these complicated feelings came up for me, about how scary the leap actually is. I realized how easy it was for me when dating, and saying what I was looking for, but the reality of what it means to step into that is actually very scary, and it feels very risky to take the step at this age, in my thirties."

She also felt some grief for the life she was giving up, including a topic for her to write about in her work. Tiffany had been single for around seven years, apart from an eighteen-month-long relationship, and it had formed a large part of what she wrote about, especially while writing her book, which explores the ten years of healing from grief and trauma following the death of her boyfriend, who took his own life while they were students at university.

"Embracing single life is so much a reaction against the stigma. You form a community and you form a belief about yourself and an identity that's in opposition to something, and I purposely sought out single friends and a lifestyle that was very fulfilling," she says. "It was also my favorite content pillar in my writing work. It was just so much a part of my work, who I was, the friendships I'd built and the life I lead. Suddenly, I realized I'd have to redefine it all. That's why I said I was leaving the single community when I told you, because it did feel like such a loss."

The accepted narrative when someone has been long-term single and then finds someone they want to be in a relationship with is that they should be both relieved and grateful. It's rare to hear someone be open about how it can feel like a loss, but it shouldn't be a surprise. Harry Levinson famously said that "all change is loss, and loss must be mourned," and I really believe this. Even if the change is hugely positive and something we have always wanted, we still lose something, and let that go in order to make space for the change. I think it's worth bearing this in mind, because all too often in life we believe we will be happy only if we reach a certain goal or milestone and then, when we reach it, we can feel a little flat. This is known as the arrival fallacy.

This is something a lot of people don't understand. When an article Tiffany wrote was published and the publication shared a post on Instagram about her views, I spotted a few negative comments that made me roll my eyes. The detractors suggested she had complained when she didn't have a boyfriend, and now complained when she did, proving once again that there is no room for nuance on social media. Overall, though, the reaction was positive. The article made people think—both those on their own and those in relationships. I am glad she published the piece, even though the relationship she was in has since ended and she has transitioned back to her single identity, because I believe everyone would benefit if we could be more honest about the losses that come with even the happiest of news.

Dealing with Other People's Reactions

One of my other interviewees, who I won't name, told me she was actually now in a relationship but had chosen not to reveal it to her followers because, for her, it's not the most important part of who she is.

"I'm very intentional about it, because I think that the highest and greatest measure of success in society is still being in a relationship or being married," she told me. "I still think we measure success that way and, as someone who is in the public eye to an extent, and someone who has a platform, I feel personally, for me, that I have a responsibility to not ever center that."

She knows what would happen if she were to post a picture with her partner to make the announcement. "It would really piss me off how many people would like it in comparison to how many people like posts when I talk about my accomplishments or my achievements. People would say things like, 'Oh my God, amazing' and 'I'm so happy you finally found this' and 'So glad you're finally happy.' In reality, I was so happy the whole time I was single, so this person coming into my life doesn't change that. Relationships should be a side note, not the main focus."

On social media, content that portrays couples statistically outperforms content of women by themselves, she points out. "We all fall into this bullshit notion of 'couple goals' and we think that's what success looks like. I think of the younger women who would look at my page and go, 'Oh, my God, she's amazing. She's done all of this and she's got a man,' which I would deeply resent. And I think I have a responsibility to them too."

This is something Angelica Malin, who edited *Unattached: Empowering Essays on Singlehood*, a book I wrote an essay for, has grappled with since announcing to her followers, just six months after the book's publication, that she was not only no longer single but also married and pregnant with her first child. She wrote for *Grazia* magazine that she felt conflicted by the reaction, as she realized that she was being more celebrated for her whirlwind transatlantic marriage and pregnancy than she was for the release of her three books and other career achievements. It made her question whether she was a good feminist.

I spoke to Sara Eckel, the author of *It's Not You*, who wrote her cult classic book (which sprang from her viral *New York Times* Modern Love essay) shortly after meeting her husband in her late thirties. It was inspired by her mainly single existence up until that point. One reason I was so keen to speak to Sara was that I read an article she wrote in *The Washington Post* about realizing that, despite writing The Book on what not to say to your single friends, she still managed to slip into making the same mistake with a single pal.

She tells me: "I have a very distinct memory of that moment. She was about forty and had never really had a boyfriend and I said, 'You'll find somebody, I know you will,' and she just looked at me like, 'Are you freaking kidding me?' I was like, 'Oh no, I have become the enemy!'"

Given she was long-term single, I wanted to know what the transition was like and what her reflections are now that she has been married for fifteen years. Sometimes I think that I've been single so long, I would really struggle to adapt to sharing my life with someone.

Sara had similar worries: "After so long being on my own, I genuinely worried I'd be bad at it when my partner and I moved in together, but it was a pretty smooth transition. People told me: 'Oh, you must be so hardened and set in your ways,' because I'd lived alone so long, but actually that wasn't the case. I was really grateful that I'd had that experience of having my space. There were times when we got on each other's nerves, but other things were easier."

I asked how people around her reacted to the news she was in a relationship. "There was kind of an ease to conversations and this absence of something, but in a good way, like, for example, when you meet people for the first time and you realize you don't have to explain yourself and you don't feel within yourself that compulsion to talk about what your deal is like.

"And no one looks at you and asks why you're married. I'd say I was married and, unlike when I used to say I was single, nobody asked what that was about. It's crazy when you think of it. Literally no one says to you, 'Oh, you're married. How come you haven't gotten divorced yet?' Nobody would do that, so they really shouldn't do it to single people."

When Stephanie Yeboah announced she had a boyfriend, she was surprised that, while most of her social media followers were happy for her, a few reacted really negatively. Stephanie, who describes herself as "a larger-fat, darker-skinned Ghanaian-British writer who advocates for fat bodies," had been chronicling the realities of her dating life to her online fans and, like Tiffany, it had formed a large part of her online identity. In 2019, she went viral when she shared a story of finding out that a man who had gone on a couple of dates with her had only dated her to win a dare for sleeping with a fat woman.

When she posted some pictures of her new boyfriend, however, there was a mass unfollowing of her Instagram account, with some feeling the need to message and tell her they were unfollowing and explain her newfound love was triggering for them. While Stephanie understands how upsetting it can be to see someone having something you desperately want, and does advocate unfollowing if you're finding things difficult, what she found hurtful was that people felt the need to tell her, and that they seemed to like her more when she shared her pain.

"The people who messaged me felt like my happiness was somehow a detriment to them," she says. "Others felt they would no longer relate because they knew me as somebody that only spoke about how negative and traumatic dating had been for me, so they wouldn't be able to relate to me anymore. With some of the messages, it almost felt like they wanted me to apologize for being in a relationship. There was a lot of entitlement."

The Cost of Not Being Single

Angelica's book of essays, *Unattached*, also raised for me something I hadn't considered. When I received a copy through the post, one of the other writers caught my eye. It was the author and broadcaster Rebecca Reid, who I knew at the time was married and had been since she was twenty-four. At first I wondered why she had been asked to contribute to a book on being single, but then I read her essay, "I'm a Little Bit Jealous of My Single Friends," and realized it was an important viewpoint to include. It's a lovely essay about spending her twenties coupled up and missing out on the things her single friends did. It's also about how misguided it is for people to assume married people are the best people to ask for advice, something she points out, as she noticed that when she got married people seemed to elevate her status and defer to her when someone needed relationship advice.

She writes:

> Where I mostly allowed myself to be carried through my late teens and early twenties on a tide of relationships, my single friends had to make conscious, considered choices about the lives they built for themselves . . . Their friendships with other women were deeper and more considered than mine because they spent more time together and allowed each other to be a priority.
>
> My friends who were single throughout their twenties had spent their time reflecting on who they were, what they really wanted, and on having and holding things they loved. While I had tried to do the same thing, I could never really have managed that same level of self-reflection or self-reliance.

Rebecca's essay made me wonder what other people missed about being single or what they were jealous of their single friends about. I decided to put the question to my followers on Twitter/X and Instagram. At first people seemed a bit shy to answer and most chose not to reply publicly, but instead send me messages. This was interesting in itself, as it made me wonder if it was all about keeping up appearances of being perfectly happy.

The messages were varied but there was a definite theme. I know some people find it patronizing when people say what they miss about single life, but I found the responses were really thoughtful and they all seemed to be said in good faith. Some of these people had been long-term singles themselves. A few people simply told me they missed "everything" about being single—and some of them confessed to me, privately, that they were trying to extricate themselves from their relationships, which is obviously not always easy when housing and joint finances come into play. Of course I also had a few who felt the need to tell me they didn't miss anything about being single. Those people didn't understand the assignment and, frankly, I do not believe them. There must be something, even a tiny thing.

A large majority said they missed the freedom that comes with being unattached, and I received lots of messages with people reminiscing about the days when they could do exactly what they pleased and when, without having to consult anyone else. Lots of people said they missed having their flat to themselves or that they missed not having to speak to someone else first thing in the morning. A few people mentioned no longer being able to book flights on a whim or make other fun plans, because they have to check in with their partner first. Others missed being included in fun activities with their single friends. One said she missed the "camaraderie with single friends," while another said his single mates still seemed to feel young, when he no longer does and he misses feeling that way. A couple of people ruefully told me they miss not having to deal with in-laws. A couple of people even missed the excitement of dating. One told me that she missed the chance to explore her sexuality. Someone said they missed the "empowerment that comes with total independence and self-reliance."

They reminded me that there is more I could do—and that we could all do—to make the most of being single, especially if one day we find ourselves attached. I don't want to look back with regrets on the things I wish I'd done while I had the chance. They reminded me to be grateful for the good things in my life, especially as lots of the things mentioned are things I do genuinely love. Sometimes we all need a little reminder to feel gratitude for what we do have. While the messages reminded me of all the great things about being single, they also reminded me that, as Tiffany found, there can be surprising costs when people say goodbye to single life. I think it's also important to ask our coupled-up friends these questions. For one thing, I think it helps to remind them they had a life before their partner, but it could also be the start of an open conversation about what it means to give up single life—and how that experience is different for everyone.

I felt reassured speaking to Sara, and all these other coupled-up people, that if the time comes for me, it's possible to not have a total lobotomy and still remember what it's like to be single. It has also given me a lot of food for thought about how society reacts when people announce they are in relationships. I know I'm just as guilty. For example, when Genevieve Roberts—who I spoke to about her decision to become a solo mum by choice to two children—introduced her new boyfriend to social media and later announced she was pregnant with her third child, I was overjoyed for her. What a beautiful love story, I thought, and having read her book, I knew that for her it was a dream come true. Everyone, including me, still loves a fairy tale.

THIRTEEN
The Single Manifesto

> "If women will not accept marriage with subjugation, nor men proffer it without, there is, there can be, no alternative. The woman who will not be ruled must live without marriage."
>
> —Susan B. Anthony

Whatever your position on being single, whether you want it to end tomorrow or you're happy on your own for the foreseeable future, I think everyone's life would be made a bit easier—including the lives of those in relationships—if we could make a few changes about how society views and treats single people. I want to begin to draw this book to a close with a few ideas on what needs to happen to achieve this. This is by no means an exhaustive list, and I know I have likely missed plenty of important things, but these are just some of the things I think would really help.

Education to Change Perception

Firstly, I would like to see change in education and in the messages that children and young people receive through books and media. I believe the single experience should be covered in sex and relationship education. I remember being a teenager and being totally obsessed with the fact I didn't have a boyfriend. I don't remember ever hearing the message at school or in the girls magazines I devoured that it was actually okay to not have a boyfriend. I never once considered a future that involved anything other than being married with children, nor do I remember any mention of a different way of living during any classes at school. Our RSE was pretty basic compared to what children are taught now, which I know now covers things like consent and healthy relationships, but while, at least, we were told about sex, which I know wasn't always the case, it was always through the lens of being in love with a long-term partner. No wonder there is so much stigma facing those whose lives look different, whether that's because they are single or gay or asexual or divorced or for some other reason.

The reason I have been thinking about this is because of reading about incels. As I've mentioned before, incel is short for "involuntary celibate," and incels are members of an online subculture of people, mainly men, who define themselves as unable to get a romantic or sexual partner despite desiring one. The movement is fueled by misogyny and abuse of women. The most annoying part of this is the word was originally coined by a woman who wanted to provide community for people who were lonely, but instead found the word getting hijacked and turned into something really ugly.

Those in the UK will have seen that incels and the "black pill movement" first really came to the public's attention when five people, including a three-year-old, were killed in a terrible shooting in Plymouth on August 12, 2021. The shooter, who doesn't deserve to be named, was a self-described incel who hated women, because no one would go out with him or have sex with him. Among the many tweets I saw about the topic on Twitter/X when it happened, was one that suggested the women of Plymouth should take responsibility, and that as a society we should make sure no young men are ever single. Aside from the rampant misogyny and victim blaming in that vile tweet, the last line made me want to throw things. Here was someone perpetuating the myth that the worst possible thing is to be single and we must not allow young men to suffer through the indignity of it. I very nearly tweeted the guy, but stopped myself because that's clearly what he wanted. It was bait and I nearly rose to it. However, I have been thinking about this notion that being single is deemed as being so terrible that people are turning to an extremist community online to find belonging. It's so disturbing.

Shortly after the attack in Plymouth, I saw that ministers want teachers in England to use RSE classes to teach children about incels. A spokesperson for the government is quoted as saying: "Schools play a crucial role in helping pupils understand the world around them, both through the RSHE curriculum—which allows for a school-led approach on teaching pupils about a range of current issues, including on incel culture—but also through their safeguarding duties, supporting staff to identify young people that may be at risk of radicalization."

I don't disagree with this approach, but shouldn't we also explore the step before incel culture and look at the root causes of it? Shouldn't we be teaching children and teenagers about how being single doesn't actually have to be the very worst thing that happens to you and introducing them to single role models, and the idea that you are just as worthy of happiness, and that you are enough even when you're on your own? I believe if more people heard these messages at a young age, it wouldn't just help young men stop being radicalized by this vile and misogynistic movement, it could also help everyone realize they don't have to stay in unhappy (or toxic!) relationships purely because they are too afraid of being on their own.

Obviously it is not the only solution to the problem, but

education is powerful, and getting these positive messages to children could potentially have a positive impact on the way single people are viewed in the future. It's not just children who could learn more, but also older students. Dr. Ketaki Chowkhani, for example, who I spoke about earlier in the book, leads the world's first ever single studies course, which I was absolutely thrilled to learn exists.

More universities should add single studies to their list of courses. Ketaki explains there are two reasons why she designed the course and why she thinks it's so important:

"We are studying singlehood as a phenomenon as it is a rising demography," she says. "More and more people are single, not just in India, but across the world and it's rising everywhere. So, firstly, it's a demography; it needs to be studied just as other demographics are. Secondly, it's a perspective on the world. In a similar way feminism is a perspective, singlehood is also a perspective. Students should be exposed to new ideas and different ways of thinking. And when they take single studies, they are pioneers as well as they are the first to study it and to write papers on it."

The Role of the Feminist Movement

I also want to take a moment to think about the feminist movement. I am a feminist—an intersectional one—but sometimes the feminist discourse really annoys me. It can be so narrow in its thinking. So much of modern feminism is concerned with women's equality within relationships, and while being mothers. I wholeheartedly support my feminist sisters who fight for those things, but it annoys me that there is still that assumption that everyone is in a relationship and that things are so binary. There are, of course, also problems with feminism not being intersectional as well.

I spoke to Karen Sugrue, a psychologist and feminist who is a prominent activist for women's rights in Ireland. In 2018, she was heavily involved in the campaign to repeal the 8th amendment to the country's constitution, allowing the government to legislate for abortion. The vote was won by a landslide. Karen is also single, following the end of a twenty-two-years-long relationship (sixteen years of which were spent married). She has two children, who are both teenagers.

Like me, Karen thinks feminism has some catching up to do:

> I think that there is a really big body of work within feminism needed to look at the messages out there requiring us to be in a relationship. It is profoundly coercive and it is profoundly supportive of the hetero-patriarchy. We're so socialized that we only belong in heterosexual binary couples. And society does, now, on the whole, accept gay people, but they also

> want them to be coupled up. It's also all tied up in capitalism.
>
> When you think about it, who benefits the most from this message being pushed that we should all be in monogamous relationships? It's men who benefit the most, because when they get a partner, that person, usually a woman, does end up doing so much of the work and the emotional labor. There is a reason why women are trained and indoctrinated from birth to think that they need to be in a relationship and it is not because it benefits them. It doesn't.

She says that if we reject that and say we actually are happy being single, we are told no, you're not, even by women who call themselves feminists.

> It's gaslighting and coercion. I've had it when I say this to my friends, who are also feminists. I'll say I love being single and I don't want to go back into a relationship and they tell me I'm just not over my breakup. I don't even argue with them, because you can't argue with that level of indoctrination. You just can't.

Structural Change and Government Policy to Tackle Inequality

Of course, so much would change if governments factored single people into policies and stopped financially propping up married couples, who are eligible for tax breaks and other benefits that singles miss out on. Bella DePaulo describes this as singlism, a word she coined that is now in the dictionary. It's not just a case of single shaming, it's the systematic, structural and institutional ways in which single people are unfairly disadvantaged, and coupled people are advantaged. This kind of singlism, she says, is built right into laws, policies and customs.

Bella says: "In the United States there are more than a thousand federal laws that benefit and protect only those who are legally married. This was actually one of the motivations to legalize single-sex marriage, but it still leaves everyone else of any gender or sexual orientation or identity who aren't married as second-class citizens."

In addition to this, there are also all the ways in which companies offer discounts and perks to couples, such as paying less for gym memberships or for travel or to attend cultural events, Bella points out. "Couples are essentially being subsidized by single people, who have to pay more—and yet it's already more expensive to be single, especially if you are living alone."

This is something, despite the name of my newsletter, that I don't dwell on too much, as it makes me want to tear my hair out, but listening to Bella makes me want to start a one-woman campaign for change. While governments who still push for everyone to get married can be voted out, organizations and companies need people to raise these things with them. I have one place I can start: for years my sister and I have pretended we live together, so that we can get the joint—and therefore cheaper—membership to a popular heritage organization, which I won't name. After speaking to Bella, I think about how absurd this is. Why can't siblings or friends get joint membership in order to save money? Why does it matter that they don't live together? Surely it would mean that more people would be able to join, and isn't that exactly what this organization wants?

When it comes to much bigger problems, such as poverty, homelessness and surviving the cost-of-living crisis, something that would help us understand the scale of the problem would be for the government to start looking at the intersection between these things and relationship status. By not collecting this data, they are able to ignore the problem and wash their hands of it. And it is a problem.

Single people are more likely to use food banks than those in relationships, recent data from the Citizens Advice Bureau showed, for example. They analyzed referrals to food banks and found that single people, and especially single people with children, are more likely to be referred, compared to couples with or without children.

Tackling the Housing Crisis

As I've mentioned previously in this book, the Women's Budget Group has repeatedly found that, thanks to women earning less than men, there is currently not a single place in the country where it is affordable for a woman earning an average income to buy or rent a home on her own. Journalist Vicky Spratt, who is the author of *Tenants*, a book where she investigates the housing crisis and the impact it has on those who rent, says the high cost of living on your own has serious consequences. There are so many ways the housing crisis could be tackled, which Vicky explores in her book and which is much more comprehensive and well researched than anything I could offer here, but I want to highlight why it's so important.

In an interview for *The Single Supplement*, Vicky said: "Women stay in relationships because they can't afford not to and I think that's a huge problem. We also know this interlinks with the issue of domestic abuse, and I mean that in the broader sense, so in terms of emotional abuse and control too. I think it's really important to consider the economics of being in a relationship or not in a relationship—and that gets overlooked."

Vicky has her own experience of how hard it can be to go from being in a relationship to being single. She first experienced living alone after the breakdown of a long-term relationship with a man she considered her life partner. It was a disorientating and expensive time. "My ex and I were not actually married, but we found that separating property was harder than getting a divorce would have been," she told me in the interview for my newsletter.

"I don't know if I was brave as it just had to happen, but financially we both took a hit and I was very scared for a very long time," she said. "I have two jobs and I love what I do, and I'm very privileged, but there is a reason I have two. It's a necessity because I am paying for a life that was once funded by two people on my own. I'm saying that quite literally, as I stayed in the home we owned together, so economics is such an important thing to talk about, particularly in a world with the gender pay gap and how extortionate housing is. For a lot of women, being in a relationship is the only way to afford certain things."

At the time of editing, some new statistics were released showing that single mothers were most likely to be impacted by no-fault evictions. Emily Morris, the author of *My Shitty Twenties*, has recently had a struggle to find a new house for her and her teenage son after getting evicted when her landlord decided to sell up. House prices had shot up while she had been living in the rented accommodation in an area of Manchester, meaning people on low incomes, like Emily, were struggling not to be priced out of the area. For some, it might seem a no-brainer to just move to a cheaper area, but those who say that don't take into consideration the distances from work and schools and the support networks people build up over time.

Emily's neighborhood has also been hit by a double-whammy of house price increases and gentrification. The monthly rent on a two-bed terraced house, the type she has always lived in with her teenage son, has risen from roughly £500 to up to £900 in the space of about five years. Even one-bedroom flats are marketed at £800 a month. These prices might not sound much to those from more expensive cities, such as London, but the increase has been sharp and cruel for local people.

"When my son goes to uni in a couple of years, I'll lose the single parent element of Universal Credit and only be able to afford a room in a house share, leaving him with no home to come back to when he needs it. I'm considering a career change, because writing books and my beloved job in a school library won't be viable for much longer," she says.

Emily would like to see real change, both on a policy level and in how the whole house-sale industry is marketed. She points out that it's harder to get a mortgage on your own. Banks would much rather lend to couples who have two incomes.

"I think the government should introduce a policy to help single people get on the housing ladder, because it feels so impossible for me right now," she says. "But it isn't just the big government policy things that get to me, it's also that there's no inclusivity in advertising and the media around housing. The stories on Rightmove are all couples talking about the coastal retreat or the Victorian terrace they are doing up and all of the imagery used on adverts about mortgages show couples and families in their adverts.

"I'd just like single people to have some recognition that we exist, because, at the moment, there's a complete lack of representation. Everywhere I look makes me feel that I'm supposed to just marry anyone in order to get ahead and have a stable housing situation."

The Cost of Having and Raising Children Alone

The question of parenthood is next on my agenda. Single parents have much lower levels of wealth than those in couples, research from the Institute of New Economic Thinking at Oxford University confirmed in 2022. This is a problem in many rich countries. In France, Italy and Spain, single-parent households were found to have just over half the average wealth of dual-parent households, while in the UK they had just 37%.

Children in single-parent families face around twice the

risk of poverty as those in couple-parent families, and single-parent households are particularly affected by employment barriers, such as the resistance some employers have toward flexible working and the lack of well-paid part-time roles. They are also particularly affected by welfare reform, such as when benefits are cut. Added to this, Britain famously has some of the most expensive childcare in the world. The annual cost of childcare has risen by £2,000 since 2010, meaning the UK now has the second-highest childcare costs among leading economies, according to the Organisation for Economic Co-operation and Development.

These are the kinds of statistics that make me think it will never be possible for me to have a baby by myself. If I do brave it, and just accept that I will financially suffer, there's still the small matter of needing to be able to afford to have treatment in the first place. In most places, treatment for single people, which can include the buying, transportation and storage of sperm, and then either artificial insemination or full-blown IVF, is not available on the NHS. Having a baby on your own can set you back tens of thousands of pounds. While heterosexual couples are expected to try to conceive for two years before accessing NHS-funded treatment, those who can't, such as single women or female same-sex couples, are expected to have had twelve cycles of artificial insemination, with at least six of the cycles using a method called intrauterine insemination (IUI), before they are eligible. As IUI costs between £350–£1,600 per cycle at a private clinic, not to mention the cost of buying sperm from reputable sperm banks, this is out of reach for a lot of people.

In 2019, NHS South East London hit the headlines when it emerged their guidelines explicitly said that only women in a "stable relationship" could access fertility treatment; "because of the known disadvantage that providing assisted conception to a single woman would cause both the child and the mother, funding of assisted conception for single women is not available."

My own local area makes no mention of single people whatsoever in its eligibility guidelines on fertility treatment. This isn't the case everywhere. There are some Scandinavian countries where single women can access government-funded IVF. In Denmark, for example, all women under the age of forty can access three free cycles of IVF, regardless of relationship status. Meanwhile, Norway gave single women access in 2020. Sadly, the list of countries that prevent single women accessing IVF treatment is longer.

A recent campaign by lesbian couple Whitney and Megan Bacon-Evans called on the government to end the barriers facing LGBTQ+ couples wanting to start a family. The government responded, as part of its long-awaited Women's Health Strategy, and pledged to remove the barriers facing lesbian couples. (It's also worth mentioning that it's even more complex for male same-sex couples, where a surrogate is needed, but as the strategy only deals with women, there is no mention of them.) When it was announced, there were rumors that the Women's Health Strategy would include a pledge for single women too, however the strategy doesn't actually specifically mention us. This is disappointing but unsurprising. Clearly there is a lot of work to be done.

What You Can Do to Change the Conversation

It's not all hopeless. There are things we can do as individuals. I think we should shout more about our experiences. We can use our voice to shift the conversation, to make people think differently about what it means to be single, to remind people that a lot of us are not actually in a relationship—and that it is totally normal and that governments around the world should stop ignoring us. This could be done in a small way, such as by sharing stories about our lives—the positive stuff and the challenges—with friends and family. If you don't want to share your own stories, you could perhaps point them toward interesting articles or TV programs that portray single people in a balanced way.

If you want to take it a step further, you could write to

the editors of your favorite magazine or the producers at your local radio station and ask them to cover the single experience more, rather than assuming their audience is all coupled-up. You could follow this up by writing to your MP, and ask for them to support policies that could improve the lives of single people. If you're a bit more open, you could brave doing a social media post about the misconceptions about single life—or maybe even put yourself forward to be interviewed for articles. (Several readers of my newsletter have recently been interviewed for articles in various publications, and for radio and television shows such as BBC Radio 4's *Woman's Hour* and Channel 4's *Steph's Packed Lunch*.)

Doing small things really does make a difference. When I appeared as a guest on Jeremy Vine's show on BBC Radio 2 to raise the issue that politicians and the media should stop saying their policies are for hardworking families when actually they are for all, I was inundated with messages from people saying they were cheering at the radio as I was speaking, or that they had sent the link to the segment to friends and family. I was especially touched by the older people who contacted me. One tweeted that they had never heard anyone speak publicly about single life before. Some of them were really emotional and I know that the producers of the show received loads of calls from people who lived alone and finally felt brave enough to share their experiences. It made me more determined than ever to keep speaking up.

Ketaki Chowkhani agrees that, as individual single people, we need to help change the conversation and suggests social media as a place to do this. Her account on Instagram is @spinster.adventures, and she also uses the hashtags #spinsteradventures and #SinglehoodGoals: "When I told my students why I started this account, the whole class started clapping. I told them that by creating the account, I was trying to make that intervention. All we see around us are images of couples and #couplegoals under pictures. Being single doesn't have that kind of image around it and it's not celebrated in the same way, hence this Instagram account and hence this hashtag. It was just a small way to try and counter the amount of couple content out there."

The more the media realize that millions of people live life solo, the more single people will be included, and this will seep into the public consciousness, which will make us feel less like total freaks of nature for not being conventional. Not everyone has questioned the way the world is designed for couples or given much thought to how society and the culture we are raised in impacts the way we behave and what we think of as the correct way of doing things. Not everyone has educated themselves or challenged their own beliefs. Not everyone has experimented with living life a bit differently. Not everyone has even been around people who don't fit the status quo.

Gandhi is often quoted as saying that we should be the change we want to see in the world. He didn't actually say these words, but what he did say has been paraphrased from a much longer quote, which is more nuanced and stresses we don't need to wait to see what others do before making changes. One of the ways we could start is by simply stopping caring what other people think and not let how others view us hold us back. I really do think one of the best ways we can make a change is to simply live our most fulfilled and best lives as single people and let that do the talking.

FOURTEEN
Living in the Gray

After I had been single for around a year, following my decision to stay single for a while, I had an evening out in Kensal Rise in northwest London with one of my best friends. It was one of those great nights where you just sit with an old friend, chattering away, putting the world to rights, and only realize that you're a bit merry when you stand up and your knees feel a bit like jelly. At some point during the evening we got onto the subject of being single. I think one of our other best mates had just got engaged, but to be honest my memory is quite hazy. After talking for a while about how far ahead everyone else seemed to be, Phoebe announced she had something positive to say. This in itself was very funny, because even though she is actually a very sweet and good-natured person, she can sometimes come across as a little pessimistic—or in her own words—cranky.

"Go on, tell me this positive thing," I said.

"Well, just think: we've still got the best bit to come," she said. "You know, how at first it's all exciting and new and you're starting to fall in love. You can't get that part back when you've been with someone ages. But we still have that to look forward to."

"Oh my God," I replied, as a warm glow seemed to fill my hopeful heart—or maybe that was just the alcohol. "You're so right. Also that actually was really positive, Pheebs. We should do a toast."

"A toast to the fact I didn't say something cranky for once?" she laughed, raising her glass.

"To Phoebe saying something positive," I said. "To the best bit being still to come!"

"Cheers!" she said, looking quite proud of herself.

It was only around a year after our night in Kensal Rise that Phoebe got to experience that new exciting feeling. I, of course, have not yet. But the conversation occasionally comes up, usually because the pictures from the evening come up on Facebook memories. It's officially known as The Time Phoebe Said Something Positive. I know Phoebe believes I still have it to come—and as much as I enjoy my single life, I do see it in my future too, and I would like it for myself. Sometimes when I think about that first bit of a relationship, I feel excited that I do still have that to come and I wonder what the person I'll feel that way about will be like.

Am I Just Kidding Myself?

But because I advocate for single people and talk a lot about finding peace with being single, sometimes I think people misinterpret me and don't understand that life is not binary. Last year, when I was hungover, sleep deprived, hormonal and had just arrived home after the wedding of a good friend, I decided to leave a voice note for another friend. Things had been distant between us for a while and I thought that telling her about my weekend and seeing how hers was would help us reconnect and get things back to normal.

At first all is well, but then I tell her about the couple's first dance. My voice shakes as I explain that, as they danced, I felt a pang of longing and thought to myself: "I want that too." Before I know it, I am crying so much that I have to ring off to calm myself down. Did I mention the fact I was hungover, had barely slept and was also getting my period?

Later I receive a voice note back, which says something along the lines of the following:

"I know you think you're happily single, but as your friend I think I've got to be honest with you: you are not happy. I know you talk about all this stuff a lot, but if you listen to what you just said, it's obvious you want to find a husband and you just need to start being honest with yourself."

At first, perhaps, because I was feeling quite vulnerable at the time, I gave her the benefit of the doubt that she was just genuinely being concerned rather than being judgmental, which is how it actually felt. The thing I find most irritating is that I have never once said I am happy being single forever and never want to find a partner, which I did point out in the message I sent back to her. Later on I began to feel quite pissed off about the message, because she seemed to have suggested that I am actually lying or deluded for talking about single life. Just because I shared one wobbly moment where I felt emotional, that, to her, immediately negated all of my previous words about the single experience. Maybe, I thought, she hadn't really been listening to me this whole time?

It's not the first time I have come up against this attitude. It's like it's impossible to simultaneously think two things at the same time: I am happy and comfortable being single, and I see myself finding a partner in the future and would like that for myself. Sometimes I feel sad that I haven't had a great love story yet. Sometimes I feel the lack of romantic love in my life keenly. Sometimes I just want someone to lean on. Sometimes I wish I could just share the burden of making huge life decisions with someone (and smaller ones, like what to eat for dinner!). But then I can go for months without ever considering what I am "lacking" and I barely think about my relationship status. Other times I can feel actively grateful that I'm doing life alone, free from having to compromise. It's complicated. It's nuanced. It can change on a day-to-day basis. A few years ago a line in a TV show summed up how I feel. The TV show in question was *Dawson's Creek*—what can I say? I love the comfort re-watching old favorites gives me. In one of the episodes Joey Potter says something that resonated so much I named this chapter after it: "For some people everything is black and white, but it's not like that for me. I live in the gray."

As I've explored, there are single people who are happy on their own and know that will never change. As Bella DePaulo calls them, they are "single at heart." Just like the women who say they don't want children are constantly told "You'll change your mind," those who want to stay single are told "You're kidding yourself." It's a shame, as a society, we can't let people who are the experts of their own lives be without automatically telling them they are wrong. So, for the record, I do believe people when they say they will remain single for life and I celebrate them for making a valid choice that suits them. I've met lots of people who feel that way. I haven't ever thought to myself: "Well, this person needs to get really honest with themselves."

Occasionally I have even wondered if I am one of them. During my interview with Bella DePaulo, I actually felt really compelled by the idea and realized I fit a lot of the criteria of what makes someone single at heart, which is what Bella studied in her research. Afterward I wondered whether being single just suited me better, and I should just accept it and lean into it. The idea didn't terrify me or make me sad, but I also didn't feel like that was the path for me. I know I would like to meet someone and experience a long-term, stable, happy relationship. I've always thought this was in my future and that it could happen for me.

Nevertheless, fearing that maybe this friend was staging an intervention and that everyone else was thinking what she was thinking about me being in denial, I told Gem, another of my married friends, about the conversation.

"But you always mention that you would like to meet someone. You've never said you want to be single forever," Gem said in response.

"Thank you," I said in relief. "I thought I was going crazy for a minute there."

"Also, everyone gets emotional at weddings. Even I do and I am not a crier."

"Yes, exactly. I've even talked in my newsletter about how much I love weddings and how I always cry at them and how I'm a massive romantic."

"Yeah, you're probably more romantic than me!"

The writer Jillian Anthony said something when I interviewed her that also rings true and makes me feel a bit more empathy for friends who say things that come across as judgmental. She said all of us are protective of who we are and our status because we feel threatened when someone comes along who is doing something completely different.

"Even if your friends are really good friends, people are still naturally really protective of their own status," she said. "I'll use myself as an example. I'm a single woman and I'm thirty-four, so a part of me feels like I have to tell myself all the good things about being single at thirty-four and all the bad things about marriage and kids. I feel like married people have to do the same thing. They don't want to think about the positives of being single. It's all about self-preservation. So your friends can still be good friends but they will naturally be thinking: 'But don't you want what I have?' and 'I have it better than you.'"

But she added that, given we live in a society that expects everyone to be in a couple, they really shouldn't feel threatened. "Everything is designed for them, so I don't feel sorry for them. They are fine."

The thing is that having wobbly moments or feeling down are part of life, no matter what your circumstances and, of course, plenty of people in relationships go through ups and downs too. Being comfortable about being single doesn't mean I'll be single forever and, likewise, feeling emotional about being alone doesn't mean I secretly hate being single and am lying to myself.

Making Space for Nuance

Early in this book I talked about a documentary on the *New York Times* website that I watched, called *35 and Single*, that transformed the way I felt about being on my own. Sometimes I return to it and give it a watch when I want to remind myself I'm not the odd one out in feeling conflicted, and also to remind myself of how far I've come since those days when I was leaping from one intense love affair to another as someone for whom self-love was a total mystery. As well as making a point about the pressure women feel to find a partner, the documentary maker, Paula Schargorodsky, also explored her mixed feelings about what she really wanted in the film.

In the voice-over, Paula says that, in your twenties, you're free to do whatever you want. You can have boyfriends, lovers and one-night stands alongside work and study, just like men do. But, she says: "Female freedom has an expiration date. When you turn thirty, a conservative curtain falls. At every social gathering you are confronted with one silent question: When will you settle down?"

A graphic on the screen pops up, it says 25% of her wanted to get married, 27% wanted to be free, 26% longed for a spiritual life and 22% wanted children. "I still don't know how to resolve this equation, but at least I learned a few things about myself. I don't want those intense impossible relationships of my twenties, nor do I want a perfect husband behind a white picket fence, and I definitely don't plan to spend my life alone," she said in the voice-over.

In the decade since I watched that film, I have done so much work to make myself stronger as a person, but, like Paula, I still haven't quite resolved the equation of all the competing things I want, yet I feel like I am getting close to solving it.

I spoke to Rachel Thompson, an editor at *Mashable* and author of *The Love Fix* and *Rough*, about how she navigates living in the gray. After a period of dating a lot and getting involved in toxic situationships, she has taken the last year off dating and is feeling good about it, adding that, as she has been single for thirteen years, it is her default state, which makes it easier.

"When I think about dating, it just feels like another chore on my to do list, which is already enormous. I find it irritating that I have to put so much effort into this thing just because society tells me that I need to be in a relationship with someone. I'm really busy and I don't have time to put as much time and energy into it as others do. For some people, it's a top priority to find a partner, but I just find the expectation really annoying."

Being single is not something that keeps her up at night, but she has moments where she worries that she'd better get a move on, adding: "The patriarchy is definitely in my brain somewhere. I've internalized that messaging around, like, your body clock is ticking and all of that stuff.

"I'm very independent and self-sufficient and I love where I'm at in my life. I'm financially secure. I live alone and I have a lovely little flat. I think it would take a lot and someone really remarkable for me to want to give up my current lifestyle," she says. "But it does change. Some days I do think about wanting a partner. Other times I panic about it but the dominant way I feel, especially in the last year, is really happy with my life and being single. I think some people who have been serial monogamists just think you must feel panicky all the time but I really don't. There isn't a lot of nuance around the subject."

Kris Hallenga also felt content with her life, but was open to whatever might come her way. She told me: "I have a life where I am surrounded by people that really care about me, and that I deeply care about. I am open to romantic love, but I just think if it doesn't come to me then the love I do have is more than enough."

But, she added: "And maybe I'm cheating a little bit because I've got a twin. We are bonded for life and we are a partnership. It's not a lover but I do have that and maybe

I would feel differently about being single if I wasn't a twin."

I've also gotten to a place where I feel confident and comfortable in myself. As I've mentioned before, this is something I am very proud of, especially given my past, but sometimes I do wonder if I am cutting my nose off to spite my face by leaning so strongly into my singleness at the expense of potentially finding the kind of love that my friends shared. My life, which has so often been chaotic and dramatic, feels pretty balanced right now. Like Paula, I don't want the intense, impossible relationships of my twenties. Or maybe what's really going on is that I'm scared to rock the boat? As comfortable as I am in my life, there could be a great payoff in getting uncomfortable too. Could it be time to make space for a romantic partner in my life and risk everything going tits up again?

Not Finding Romantic Love

I also know that some people do not find this kind of love. Some people remain single, not because they haven't opened their arms up to it like Bella, but because they haven't been able to find someone compatible. I think it's important to talk about this because it feels like a bit of a taboo. If all the motivational Instagram posts and articles on dating and books on finding love and not getting stuck in the single trap were to be believed without question, there would definitely be someone out there for everyone. "You will find someone," they chorus. "It will happen when you least expect it," some say, while others shout about treating dating like a part-time job. Hardly anything I've read acknowledges that actually some people will not find romantic love. That's just a fact and I do think we should shine a light a bit more on how it feels when things don't work out how society expects, because those experiences are valid.

This is something writer and director Aimée Lutkin explored in her memoir, *The Lonely Hunter.* It begins as she recounts a conversation she had at a dinner party in New York City, where she lives. As she was enjoying the meal, Aimée's friends asked the question that all singles are familiar with: "So, what's going on with your love life?" In a moment of vulnerability, she admitted nothing was going on with her love life and nothing had been going on for quite some time.

She then voiced her deep suspicion that she might end up being alone forever. Her friends rolled their eyes immediately and then actually seemed to get annoyed with her. They insisted that she would eventually meet someone because everybody does and that she just had to wait for it and be patient and not give up.

"People seem to have this thing where they assume that,

because they have that, anyone can have it," she told me in an interview for this book. She went on to say:

> Love can feel really random. It can feel like this magical thing that's happened to you. And I think we tell the story of it being destiny and of it being inevitable a lot. We tell this story that love is something that will eventually find everybody but it's just not reality. The possibility exists for anybody but it's not guaranteed by a long shot.
>
> I don't think most people in relationships would admit this, but I do think that if you're in a relationship, there is a subset of people who think that they've earned it somehow by being good. There's a moral superiority to it and there is this assumption that if you can't find it, then there's something you need to work on to make yourself worthy of it.
>
> When you suggest that you might never meet somebody to someone who's in a relationship, I think a part of them recognizes that as a threat, because they could lose the love that they have. The person could die. They could leave them. Anything could happen. Love is not guaranteed, and it's not forever.

Although I am a romantic, I've met enough people now to know that life never really works out how we think it might. Like Aimée says, we can't guarantee anything, so I'm realistic that I may actually end up single for life, just like I know that I may end up never having a child. Or it may not happen for a long time. Maybe I'll be ninety when I finally meet someone who I fall into safe, secure love with.

What I've Learned While Writing This Book

As this book draws to its close, I have been reflecting on the roller coaster of emotions I've been through since I first began to work on it. Some of the interviews have left me punching the air and wanting to gather all my single friends together and howl at the moon or do something equally wild and free. Others have made me cry and really confront the things I find hardest to think about. It's probably no surprise, but the interviews I found the hardest were about motherhood. In the world of journalism, you're taught to hold your emotions in during interviews, but that felt wrong for this, and so I sometimes cried along with my interviewees unashamedly, and I think our conversations were richer for it. I also laughed an awful lot, and nodded my head so many times in some of the interviews I thought my head might roll off my body.

Most of the interviews left me feeling happier than ever about being single, but of course, even when you're holed up working on a project like this, life goes on all around you and other things have the power to make you think differently. A lot has happened since I first began working on this. Close friends I thought I would be around forever have disappeared from my life. Family members have had terrifying health scares. People I love have struggled with mental illness and my own mental health has also, at times, been poor. Friends have gotten pregnant and had babies, and I've felt that familiar feeling of happiness for them and pang of grief for me. I've seen heartbreaking, life-changing loss up close.

It was actually after my friend's funeral that I felt the most longing for a relationship since first becoming single. Sitting in that church, which was packed to the rafters, and hearing about the love she and her husband had for each other, made me realize how precious that really is. Far from putting me off, as I know some people are when they encounter this level of heartbreak, it had the opposite effect. I wanted that kind of love for myself even if it was to be cruelly cut short. It's better to have loved and lost, as the saying goes. My former passionate, intense love affairs were in no way comparable, I realized.

At the end of Oliver Burkeman's book *Four Thousand Weeks*, he poses five questions to help people consider what's important to them and how they want to prioritize their time. One of them is this: "Where in your life or work are you currently pursuing comfort when what's called for is a little discomfort?" This made me think about how even though my twenties were a decade of upheaval, the best part of them was the sense of adventure I had and the way I was always forcing myself out of my comfort zone to try new things.

In my mid-twenties, when I lived in Spain, I remember telling my landlord, an elderly Basque man, that I'd decided on a whim to get an overnight bus to the other side of the country that night in order to spend my week's holiday volunteering on a small organic orchard in exchange for free food and board. It was not the first spontaneous and quite random thing I'd done since moving in. After looking at me quizzically for a long time, he finally nodded and said: "Ah . . . you are an adventurer!" I loved it not because of the physical adventure I was about to undertake but what he had realized about me, which was about who I was at the core. I felt like he had looked into my soul.

While I was able to hang on to my adventurous side well into my thirties, I have somewhat lost it in recent years. The pandemic and the emotional fallout of it, which I think will take us many years to really face up to, plus a sudden inexplicable urge to be financially secure and sensible after years of not caring a jot (which I assume is down to aging), are things that have contributed to keeping me small. I think, also, finally facing up to my trauma has made me wince at how reckless I was in the years following that relationship, when I didn't care about myself and wanted to press self-destruct. When you finally learn to care about yourself and you realize just how much of a gift life is, you want to keep yourself nice and safe and comfortable, as I have been for the last few years.

Speaking to all the people I've spoken to for this book and excavating my mind and memories for all the stories I've told in these pages has really reminded me that I am still that adventurer the Spanish man recognized all those years ago. Whatever my next adventure entails, whether that's solo motherhood or meeting someone I feel safe with who loves me as much as I love them, I am ready for it. Or maybe it will end up being a totally different adventure, one that I haven't even dreamed of yet. That's an exciting thought.

Conclusion: Life Lessons from a Decade of Singledom

At the time of writing, I have been single for ten years. I had no idea when I decided to temporarily remove myself from the dating pool that I wouldn't call another person "boyfriend" for a whole decade. As I've explored in these pages, the experience has been a roller coaster, with wild highs and depressing lows, but there has also been so much joy and fulfilment.

Here's what I wish I had known a decade ago:

You have just made the best decision of your life. You're at the start of developing a relationship with the most important person you'll ever get to know. That person is you. You may be twenty-nine, but between all the bad mistakes and broken hearts, you actually don't know yourself very well at all. You've been hiding in all the drama and getting all your validation from boys whose opinion you really shouldn't have valued so much.

Please know this: you're not a failure. There is nothing wrong with who you are as a person. Your value as a human being does not depend on your relationship status. You don't need a man to tell you your value. Deep down, you already know it. Lean into that.

It is actually possible to be single and happy. I'm serious. You really will find happiness even when you're alone. People will doubt you. Those people are small-minded and probably secretly miserable themselves and are just projecting it onto you. Let yourself feel happiness. Choose joy. Have fun. Prioritize pleasure.

Treasure your friends. They are precious and they will have your back in ways you can't even imagine now. Don't just have "catch-ups." Make new memories with your old friends. Spend time with their children and/or partners, but also spend time together without them doing fun things, like jumping into waterfalls and going to gigs of bands you loved when you were in your teens.

Equally, allow yourself to make new friends, especially single ones or people who don't fit the status quo. Find your tribe. Making new friends doesn't mean you love your coupled-up friends any less. You just sometimes need to surround yourself with people who "get it," especially if you are single at a time when every other person on the planet seems to be getting engaged and having babies.

Bulk buy toilet roll and tea bags. When you live alone, you won't be able to blame anyone else if you forget to buy them and run out at an inconvenient moment, so do yourself a favor and stock up on essentials.

Do something really spontaneous whenever you get the urge. Revel in the freedom. This is what coupled-up people miss the most from their single life. I know, because hundreds of them told me so when I asked on social media. When you realize you have a month off work to fill, jump on a plane to Morocco. It will be your greatest adventure.

You're not really in love with your friend. You will have to learn this lesson a few more times. That's okay. Sometimes you have to keep making the same mistake until you really get it. It just feels safer to say you love him because you know, deep down, that a) you don't really feel that way, so your heart is protected and b) he definitely doesn't either, but you both get an ego boost from flirting with each other.

While we're on the topic, a boy will come along when you've been single for a long time and you will feel that instant magic chemistry and it will feel oh so familiar. That's because he's basically a carbon copy of your ex. I would advise you to avoid him, but I'm pleased to say you swerved disaster all on your own this time—thanks to learning a thing called self-respect—so you may as well enjoy all the outrageous flirting until you get there.

There will be shit times. Sometimes it will feel like everything is going wrong. Hang in there. You will survive and you will end up feeling stronger and more resilient than ever.

Be honest with your friends. Don't try to pretend you don't care about stuff when you do. More often than not, people just haven't considered how life is different when you're on your own and how it feels to be The Last Single Girl. Not everyone will want to hear your honesty—they will get defensive and weird—but the ones that do are the keepers.

Life is short. In time you will begin to lose people who are far too young to die and each time it will hit you like a ton of bricks that you can't sit around waiting for your life to start. This is your life. Make the most of it. To steal my parents' favorite motto: "One Life. Live it."

You don't have to love yourself before anyone else will. You are lovable just the way you are and you deserve love no matter how messed up you feel inside. Besides, love doesn't just mean romantic love. You are already surrounded by love.

Having said that, learning to love and accept yourself will be the best lesson of your life. But do it for yourself, not to make yourself more appealing to the other sex.

In general, be more Cristina Yang. Take her words from *Grey's Anatomy* to heart: "Be unstoppable. Be a force of nature. Be better than anyone here and don't give a damn about what anyone thinks."

Do yourself a favor and listen to Tola Fisher when she tells you to get income protection insurance.

Finally, no one is coming to rescue you. You have to rescue yourself. And you will.

Epilogue

After I finished the second draft of this book and moved toward the more detailed part of the editing process, I was making a huge decision. Maybe it was writing the book that made me realize what I needed to do. Maybe it was finishing the book that gave me permission. I don't know. I only know this book and what happened next are intertwined. It began in the new year, just weeks after I finished the first draft. I decided 2023 was the year I was going to do something about having a baby. After years and years and years of longing and confusion and feeling—for want of a better word—paralyzed by fear, I suddenly felt compelled to take action.

While mulling this over and editing this book, a few things happened all in the same week. Firstly, I went to see SELF ESTEEM, as documented in this book, and during the song "You Forever," I realized I needed to be braver in my life. I've played this song a hundred times at home, but something about hearing it live made a difference, and I took those words to heart. Another part of the song jumped out about how we do such a lot of "longing" and very little "living." Oof. That felt like the last three years of my life. I do need to be braver, a lot braver, I thought.

Shortly after this a friend in a serious relationship found out her boyfriend was cheating on her. Not only was she grieving the loss of her love but also the future they'd planned together, which included becoming parents. As someone who is five years older than her, I knew I couldn't risk this happening to me. I could not let some dickhead masquerading as a committed boyfriend waste my final years of fertility only for it all to crash and burn. Secondly, in a WhatsApp group I'm in for people considering solo motherhood, one of the group, who is around five years older than me, had her final failed round of IVF and accepted she may never be able to get pregnant. When she messaged us, she included a warning: "If you're thinking about it, just do it. Don't leave it too late like I did."

Later that week, the government announced they were going to bring in free childcare hours for younger babies—which although not perfect, was a good signal that the issue was being taken seriously. The cost of childcare was making my head spin, so the news was incredibly welcome. That's it, I thought, when I saw the headlines. It's a sign. I'm going to try to have a baby. That Friday, I braved telling my mum. At first I said I was going to get a fertility test and then I said I was considering solo motherhood with a sperm donor. We had a heart to heart and she was fully on board and supportive, but, also, concerned about how I would manage financially and practically on my own. For the next few weeks I told her I was going to call the fertility clinic but kept putting it off. The reason was that I had another idea. A secret idea.

Two weeks after telling my mum I was thinking of going it alone, I got incredibly drunk with my friend Tom—the one who I'd spent New Year's Eve dancing with, which I wrote about in an earlier chapter—and asked if he'd like to platonically co-parent a child with me. It was the scariest thing I've ever asked anyone, but I'd been researching the idea for a while, after meeting a woman five years previously who, along with her wife, was platonically co-parenting with a single gay man. None of my other gay friends seemed to fit the bill, but then I met Tom in 2020. He says that, as soon as we met, he knew I was going to play an important role in his life and I felt the same way. We had just clicked.

I began to seriously consider him as a potential co-parent in the summer of 2022, and essentially spent the next eight months or so subtly interviewing Tom for the role, even though I was scared to admit even to myself that it was the route I most wanted to take. I would sometimes joke about it with my best friends, but I didn't know if I'd ever actually ask him. But in those weeks while I was avoiding calling the clinic, I realized it was what I really wanted. I also sensed he would say yes if only I could muster the courage to actually ask the question. I knew he longed to have a child and had been looking into solo fostering and adoption, as he'd given up hope of being a biological dad.

Of course, he did say yes. In fact, he says he knew what I was going to ask before I did it—and also knew that he'd say yes if I did. I clearly hadn't been as subtle as I thought. Following the initial chat, we spent three months or so having intense conversations about everything, including all the ways it could go wrong, before deciding to go for it. After the wilderness years, where I thought it might never happen, I was suddenly doing things like peeing on ovulation sticks and reading books about fertility. I couldn't believe it. I felt in awe.

Just before we started trying—using the "turkey baster method" of conception—I sent him the track "Brighter Days"—the one that Annie Mac played on New Year's Eve 2020 when I was walking the streets alone. As a lover of house music, he was an immediate fan, later texting me "Brighter days are ahead Mama Slawson." He was so right.

Dear reader, I'm writing this while pregnant. Our baby is due almost exactly one year after I got drunk and pulled Tom aside in a pub and told him I had something to ask him. When we found out, we danced around his living room to "Brighter Days" to celebrate. We have been so lucky, and we know just how privileged we are to experience this. Every day I wake up and simply cannot believe that it's finally my turn. And that soft toy bunny I bought in the US all those years ago? It's now sitting proudly in the baby's toy basket, and I'm living for the day my baby finally clutches it in their tiny hands.

It sounds like a cliché, but if this story proves anything, it's that you have absolutely no idea what is round the corner. I've just re-read the lines of the final chapter of this book. I had no idea how true they would be when I wrote them. I'm now living a dream that I didn't even dare to really let myself dream. All I had to do was be a little braver, let go of what society says my life should look like and not be afraid to do things my own way. I can only hope, no matter if you are single for a day or for decades, that you can do the same.

and when we found out [illegible] around [illegible] flying [illegible] "Mystery Drops" to new [illegible]. We have been so lucky, and we know just how privileged we are to experience this. Every day I wake up and simply cannot believe that [illegible] my [illegible] [illegible] in the [illegible] years ago [illegible] the [illegible] and [illegible] for the day my [illegible] in their own hands.

It sounds like a [illegible], but [illegible] all [illegible] the corner. [illegible] the [illegible] of the book [illegible] they would [illegible] wrote them. I'm now living a dream that I didn't [illegible] to [illegible]. All [illegible] life, however [illegible] says [illegible] life should look like and not be afraid to [illegible] [illegible] no matter [illegible] that you can [illegible].

Selected Bibliography

Alderton, Dolly, *Dear Dolly: On Love, Life and Friendship* (Fig Tree, 2022)

Angel, Katherine, *Tomorrow Sex Will Be Good Again: Women and Desire in the Age of Consent* (Verso, 2021)

Azmat, Sadia, *Sex Bomb: A Memoir: The Life and Loves of an Asian Babe* (Headline, 2022)

Bolick, Kate, *Spinster: Making a Life of One's Own* (Crown Publishing Group, 2015)

Burkeman, Oliver, *Four Thousand Weeks: Time Management for Mortals* (Allen Lane, 2021)

Cohen, Claire, *BFF?: The Truth About Female Friendship* (Bantam Press, 2022)

Coontz, Stephanie, *Marriage, a History: From Obedience to Intimacy or How Love Conquered Marriage* (Viking, 2005)

Craggs, Charlie, *To My Trans Sisters* (Jessica Kingsley Publishers, 2017)

Day, Jody, *Living the Life Unexpected: How to Find Hope, Meaning and a Fulfilling Future Without Children* (Bluebird, 2020)

Dolan, Paul, *Happy Ever After: A Radical New Approach to Living Well* (Allen Lane, 2019)

Eckel, Sara, *It's Not You: 27 (Wrong) Reasons You're Single* (Penguin Publishing Group, 2014)

El-Wardany, Salma, *These Impossible Things* (Trapeze, 2022)

Fisher, Tola Doll, *Still Standing: 100 Lessons From An "Unsuccessful" Life* (SPCK Publishing, 2020)

Frizzell, Nell, *The Panic Years: Dates, Doubts and the Mother of All Decisions* (Bantam Press, 2021)

Gray, Catherine, *The Unexpected Joy of Being Single* (Aster, 2018)

Hallenga, Kris, *Glittering a Turd: How Surviving the Unsurvivable Taught Me to Live* (unbound, 2021)

Heti, Sheila, *Motherhood* (Henry Holt & Co, 2018)

hooks, bell, *All About Love: New Visions* (William Morrow & Co, 2000)

Humphries, Rebecca, *Why Did You Stay?: A Memoir About Self-worth* (Sphere, 2022)

Lamott, Anne, *Bird by Bird: Instructions on Writing and Life* (Canongate Canons, 2020)

Lawton, Georgina, *Black Girls Take World: The Travel Bible for Black Women with Boundless Wanderlust* (QUBM4, 2021)

Lord, Annie, *Notes on Heartbreak* (Trapeze, 2022)

Lutkin, Aimée, *The Lonely Hunter: How Our Search for Love Is Broken* (Scribe, 2022)

Malin, Angelica (ed.), *Unattached: Empowering Essays on Singlehood* (Square Peg, 2022)

Morris, Emily, *My Shitty Twenties: A Memoir* (Salt Publishing, 2017)

Philippou, Tiffany, *Totally Fine (And Other Lies I've Told Myself): What My Decade in Grief Taught Me About Life* (Thread, 2022)

Price, Laura, *Single Bald Female* (Macmillan, 2022)

Roberts, Genevieve, *Going Solo: My Choice to Become a Single Mother Using a Donor* (Piatkus, 2019)

Silver, Shani, *A Single Revolution* (Atta Girl Press, 2021)

Specter, Francesca, *Alonement: How to Be Alone and Absolutely Own It* (Quercus Publishing, 2021)

Spratt, Vicky, *Tenants: The People on the Frontline of Britain's Housing Emergency* (Profile Books, 2022)

Thompson, Rachel, *Rough: How Violence Has Found Its Way into the Bedroom and What We Can Do About It* (Square Peg, 2021)

Thorn, Helen, *Get Divorced, Be Happy: How Becoming Single Turned Out to Be My Happily Ever After* (Vermilion, 2021)

Thorne, Liv, *Liv's Alone: Amateur Adventures in Single Motherhood* (Hodder & Stoughton, 2021)

Traister, Rebecca, *All the Single Ladies: Unmarried Women and the Rise of an Independent Nation* (Simon & Schuster, 2016)

Selected Bibliography

Webster, Lucy, *The View from Down Here: Life as a Young Disabled Woman* (Dorling Kindersley, 2023)

Wilby, Rosie, *The Breakup Monologues: The Unexpected Joy of Heartbreak* (Green Tree, 2021)

Acknowledgments

My favorite thing to do when I get a new book is to skip straight to the acknowledgments, so it thrills me to be writing my own. Like the aspiring actors who practice their Oscar's speeches in the shower, I've been "writing" my acknowledgments in my head long before I actually got a book deal. Hopefully I'll do those who need thanking justice, because so many people have played a part in making sure this book has a birthday.

Biggest thanks must go to my amazing agent, Zoe Ross. I'm so grateful that you were able to work your magic to make my dream come true—honestly, there was some kind of wizardry to the process and I was in awe. Huge thanks also to Olivia Davies, for being so great when she stepped in, and for being there for me during the lowest moment of the process for me. I'm so proud to be part of the United family.

Huge thank you to Anna Steadman, without whom this book would still just be a proposal. Thanks for all the enthusiasm and encouragement during the latter stages of the editing process when I was flagging. And huge thanks to Zoe Blanc, for stepping in to be my editor during the early stages. Your insight and positivity made a big difference. Thanks to everyone else at Headline for your help.

Massive thanks to Amy Sun for the biggest confidence boost of my life, and the best letter I've ever received. I hope it's not too embarrassing to admit I printed it off and pinned it to my wall above my desk. It will never not make me smile. Thank you for giving me the space to make this book the best version of itself and knowing when I could push myself to improve it more. Thanks to everyone else at Penguin in the US for their support.

Thanks to Sian Curtis-Golds at Adavirtual for being my right-hand woman and helping me organize all the interviews. You're the best!

Thanks to every single person who gave up their time to let me interview them for this book. Your stories, your insight and your vulnerability have lifted this book and made it so special. Speaking to you all has been the absolute highlight of this experience. Special thanks to Paula Schargorodsky, whose documentary *35 and Single* changed my life.

Big love to all those who gave me endorsements for my proposal: Daisy Buchanan, Natasha Lunn, Heidi Scrimgeour, Nancy Groves, Emma Winterschladen, and particularly to Katherine May, who believed in this book long before I did and whose reaction to my news was essentially "it's about time."

Thanks again to Nancy and Amy Packham, and everyone else at *HuffPost* Life, for convincing me to write my first ever personal essay on being single. None of this would have happened without that first Group Chat column.

Big thanks to Lizzie Cernik, who twice landed me with thousands of extra subscribers when she mentioned my newsletter in *Guardian* articles. And thanks to everyone else who has ever interviewed me or recommended my newsletter, especially Shani Silver, who had me on her podcast not long after I launched. Thank you to the editors who commission me, but especially Max Benwell from *The Guardian* US for giving me the best ever freelance gig, and thanks to everyone at *The Guardian* UK (especially Su Haire) for keeping me solvent.

Writing this book—and even getting the book deal—was no walk in the park, not least because I have ADHD and because I don't have a trust fund or husband, obviously, supporting me financially. There were periods where I thought that deciding to write a book was the very worst idea I ever had. A lot of people have held my hand on this roller coaster and I want to thank them now.

First and foremost, big thanks to London Writers' Salon for being the very best writing community in the world. Matt and Parul: I'm so grateful. There is no way I could have done this without LWS being there for me at every single step of the journey. Thank you to each and every member of the community. It has been an honor to write alongside you in Writers' Hour and in the virtual cabin. Special thanks to all my fellow goldies. There are too many others to mention, but I have to squeeze in Lindsey Trout Hughes and Niamh Mulvey in particular for their coaching. Biggest love to the Feelings café group, who read parts of this book before anyone else, but especially Susannah Rigg for reading more than anyone else and always nudging me to tell my "truthiest" truth.

Big love to my other writing friends, who have been on the receiving end of voice notes and panicked messages. I love you so much, Emma W (again), Tiffany Philippou, Tahmina Begum, Lou Minns (and the other Shrewsbury writers!), Portia Holdsworth, Rachel Hills and James Dixon.

Aside from the virtual sessions with LWS, I wrote a lot of this book in Shrewsbury's gorgeous library and the Shrewsbury Coffeehouse. To the latter, thanks for being the loveliest team and for not minding me occupying a table for hours at a time.

Special thanks and biggest love to my family for all their support. Thanks to my mum, Edel, and dad, Andy, for teaching me to read (with Winnie the Pooh) and then encouraging me to read anything and everything I could get my hands on. Thanks also for encouraging my writing by buying me my first diary at age eight, and all the years after that. Huge thanks to my sister Rachel for being the best cheerleader and for helping me run *The Single Supplement* community! Your support means so much to me. Big love to my other family members, but particularly my uncle Rory for his great advice, and my cousin Lily for always being so excited for me and for the Ider songs that were my writing soundtrack. And, finally, endless gratitude and love to my chosen family—Tom for telling anyone and everyone about this book and, more importantly, for making my biggest ever dream come true, which also made the end of this book so magical, and, of course, to this baby bean for keeping me company in my tummy during the final stages of editing. I cannot believe my luck.

As mentioned in the pages of this book, my friends are the loves of my life. Thank you to all of them, but especially Gemma for putting up with me for nearly thirty years, being so supportive of this book and for bringing Lyla into my life; Ellen, for being one of the best people I've ever met and for always being there for me in my hour of need (and all my other friends at The Hive, an arts center in Shrewsbury, where I am a trustee); my OG uni friends, but in particular Becky P, for sending me an email that meant more than she could have known and for always being so supportive of *The Single Supplement* and not forgetting what it's like; Molly and Charlie for always accepting me for who I am; Bryony for believing in me, which means so much because it's still her opinion I value the most; Steph, Alice and the rest of the Shrewsbury gang for making nights off writing so fun and always making me feel included; Kate for giving me a talking-to during two of my lowest moments; my best faraway friend, Jade, for reminding me how important it is to celebrate our achievements, especially when our lives look different to others (and her sister, Jess, for the publishing intel and encouragement); Jo for reminding me to dream big and not hold myself back; Tanveer and Miranda for two of the best reactions to my news, when all things were confirmed; to the two Becky Bs in my life for all the support; and, finally, all my *Positive News*, *HuffPost* and *Guardian* friends, past and present.

It's around here in other authors' acknowledgments that they write that they couldn't have finished their books without their partner and they then proceed to thank them for endless cups of tea, for feeding them and for keeping them afloat while they followed their dreams. Given I don't have a partner to thank, I'm going to take this opportunity to give myself a pat on the back for the endless cups of tea I've made myself, for feeding myself while writing this and paying all my own goddamn bills. Go me!

I had to save the most important thanks to last, though. To all the readers of *The Single Supplement*, past and present, I cannot thank you enough. There would be no book without you. You have changed my life. Thank you for encouraging me, challenging me, sharing my work and looking after each other. Special thanks to all my paying subscribers: you are absolute legends and kept me going. I couldn't have asked for a better audience and community. I really hope you like this book, because it is for you.

Finally, I want to take a moment to honor the beautiful and kind Stephanie Beesley, who tragically died far too young while I was writing this book. Later in this book's journey, the amazing Kris Hallenga, who I was honored to interview for this project, also passed away. Their loss is a painful reminder that every extra day we get on this earth is a precious gift. I promise not to take that for granted and would like to invite readers of this book to do the same, whatever your relationship status.

The Single Supplement

The Single Supplement is an award-winning newsletter on Substack, especially for single people. It was launched in 2019 in response to the lack of quality content in magazines, newspapers and on social media for those not in relationships, as everything at the time assumed all single people were miserable and/or desperate to find someone. Expect musings on all aspects of single life, interviews with high-profile single people, guest writers and lots of recommendations for books, articles and podcasts.

Sign up at https://thesinglesupplement.substack.com.